Women, War & Hypocrites

Women, War & Hypocrites

Hypocrites

STUDYING THE QUR'AN

ROBERT A. CAMPBELL

Cape Breton University Press
Sydney, Nova Scotia, Canada

Cape Breton University Press recognizes the support of the Canada Council for the Arts, Block
Grant program, and the Province of Nova Scotia, through the Department of Tourism, Culture
and Heritage, for our publishing program. We are
pleased to work in partnership with these bodies
to develop and promote our cultural resources.

Layout and Cover: Barry Gabriel, South Bar, NS
First printed in Canada on 100% recycled postconsumer fibre, certified EcoLogo
and processed chlorine free, manufactured using biogas energy.

Library and Archives Canada Cataloguing in Publication

Campbell, Robert A. (Robert Arthur), 1952-
    Women, war & hypocrites: studying the Qur'an/Robert A. Campbell.

Includes bibliographical references.
ISBN 978-1-897009-53-6

    1. Koran. Sūrat al-Nisā'--Criticism, interpretation, etc. 2. Koran--Herme-
neutics. 3. Koran--Reading. 4. Islam. I. Title.

BP128.23.C35 2010   297.1'229   C2010-905443-1

Cape Breton University Press
P.O. Box 5300
Sydney, Nova Scotia B1P 6L2 CA
www.cbu.ca/press

Mixed Sources
Product group from well-managed forests,
controlled sources and recycled wood or fiber
www.fsc.org Cert no. SW-COC-000952
© 1996 Forest Stewardship Council
FSC

Contents

Acknowledgements vii

Text and Context 1
    Introduction 1
    Studying the Qur'an 11
    Shariah 46
    The Fourth Surah 56

Women 67
    Introduction 67
    Marriage 74
    Lewdness 90
    Wife Beating 94
    Hijab 124

War 131
    Introduction 131
    Killing 137
    Battle 141
    Jihad 156
    Terrorism 160

Hypocrites 171
    Introduction 171
    Believers 177
    People of the Book 189
    Idolatry 195
    Intoxication 200
    The Crucifixion of Jesus 206

Bibliography 211

Index of Subjects 225

Acknowledgments

This book reflects my continued efforts to understand Islam's sacred book, in light of the questions and concerns that have been brought to me by my students and others, and in response to what I see happening at the interface between religion and politics around the globe.

I am grateful to those who support me as I articulate my struggle through writing about the Qur'an, especially Mike Hunter and Cape Breton University Press for agreeing to publish a second book by me on the subject.

Thanks to Carla White for preparing the index, and thanks again to Barry Gabriel for the cover design and the layout of the book.

Robert Campbell
Sydney, Nova Scotia
December 2010

Text and Context

Introduction

The ultimate source of authority on all matters in Islam is the Qur'an, a text that Muslims believe was revealed by God in Arabic through the angel Gabriel to the Prophet Muhammad over a period of twenty-odd years more than fourteen hundred years ago. Given the centrality of this text to Islam and the fact that the number of Muslims in the world is around the 1.5 billion mark and growing rapidly, one would anticipate the existence of libraries full of commentaries, guidebooks, primers and concordances devoted to elucidating the contents of this sacred text and to helping people apply the lessons contained in the Qur'an to their daily lives. To some extent this is the case. Given the nature of the Qur'an and the theology of the book that has developed around it, however, one finds that for the most part these secondary works are in Arabic; their style and content adhere to strict conventions and principles many centuries old. That is only part of the story.

As Ingrid Mattson indicates, "the Qur'an has retained its prominence in Muslim societies not primarily because it has been studied and transmitted in schools and seminaries, but because it is at the center of ritual life" (2008: 106). For the vast majority of Muslims, the Qur'an is an object of reverence; its contents are to be memorized and recited as part of prayer, and as part of virtually every other activity in which a person might engage. For the devout Muslim, to study the Qur'an means (more than memorization) to learn more of its language and literal content, to become immersed in the text as a spiritual quest. The idea that the Qur'an could be subjected to systematic objective analysis is viewed by many Muslims as tantamount to desecration, comparable to the act of physically touching the Qur'an in a state of impurity. Irrespective of its status as a sacred text, however, the Qur'an is, nonetheless, a text; as such its content continues to be cited, interpreted and applied in countless situations and circumstances. Those who are unwilling or unable to delve into the text of the Qur'an on their own will always be at risk of having their opinions shaped by others, others whose intentions might not always be clear.

It is not my intention either to confirm or deny the sacred status of the Qur'an. The fact that one-fifth of the world's population believes that the Qur'an is the word of God is an adequate justification for me to be interested in learning more about this text, and to be concerned about how the text is being applied in matters of religion, politics, human rights and social welfare. What I wanted to know, and what I think others are interested in finding out, is the extent to which the actual content of the Qur'an forms a basis for the beliefs and actions of today's Muslims. Clearly, pursuing this agenda requires reading the Qur'an, and one immediate hurdle to such a pursuit is that, doctrinally, the Qur'an is considered to be the Qur'an only in its Arabic form. All translations are considered to be interpretations, and thus not capable of transmitting God's pure and true message. However, as the focus of my inquiry was not on the idea and use of the Qur'an as a sacred object, I began my exploration from the position that a fairly sophisticated level of understanding about much of the content and intent of the Qur'an can be acquired by those who can only read the text in translation. And this is the approach that I recommend to others, whether Muslim or non-Muslim. I do want to raise two notes of caution, however.

First, a great deal of the content of the Qur'an will be familiar to those with even passing exposure to the scripture of the Jews and Christians—whether this was acquired through their own religious practice or through the unavoidable and ubiquitous presence of biblical stories and themes in the canon of Western literature and in nearly every aspect of traditional and popular culture in the West, if not the globe. Given the fact that Islam traces its prophetic heritage from Noah through to Abraham, Moses, Jesus and finally Muhammad, and that the Qur'an recognizes the Torah, the Gospel and the Psalms as prior revelations, we should be surprised if we did *not* find a great deal of common material. As I maintained throughout my previous book (Campbell 2009), efforts to understand the Qur'an and Islam as emerging in a vacuum or in a context of pagan idolatry and tribal traditions are misguided. The Arabs of Makkah and the surrounding region had Christian and Jewish neighbours and trading partners; it only makes sense that worldviews would have been traded along with worldly goods. This position does not amount to a reductionist view of the Qur'an and Islam as derivative or defective copies of either Christian (Bell 1926) or Jewish (Torrey 1933) precursors, replete with numerous errors and omissions. On the contrary, frequent parallels as well as substantial differences should be expected. The important point is that every effort should be made to read the Qur'an on its own terms.

Second, and in a similar vein, a concerted effort should be made to separate what you read in the Qur'an from what you think you have learned about the Qur'an and Islam through media coverage of current events. As Sumbul Ali-Karamali expresses it: "Ludicrously unbalanced and fanatical characterizations of Islam in the media have been an increasingly insurmountable obstacle in an attempt to understand it" (2008: 218). Certainly since 9/11, not only has media attention on Islam reached unprecedented levels, a plethora of books have been written trying to present alternate understandings of Islam's past and present, especially with respect to Islam's relationship with the West. While some authors unapologetically set out to condemn Islam (Crimp and Richardson 2008; Ibn Warraq 1995; Spencer 2005), others make valiant attempts to uncover and reclaim a glorious past for Islam, based on the premise that the West would not be what it is today without the contribution of long forgotten Muslim artisans, scientists and thinkers (Menocal 2003; Morgan 2007; Wallace-Murphy 2006). For example, in the introduction to *Lost History*, Morgan states: "This book is not about Islam or any other religion. It is not about theology or religious doctrine. It is about a civilization in which Islam had a leading role" (2007: xv). The extent to which these initiatives might be viewed as disingenuous is an open question. At the very least, however, whether pro or con these efforts are often seriously hampered by an overly simplistic and monolithic view of Islam and the West as distinct identifiable entities. Again, the critical issue is to keep an open mind and to carry out your own exploration of the Qur'an and of Islam.

IN HIS BRIEF study of selected passages from the Qur'an, Mustansir Mir suggests that the three principle themes of the Qur'an are monotheism, prophecy and the afterlife (2008: 15). Certainly it is difficult to imagine anyone contesting the fact that monotheism is the central theological focus of the Qur'an, but as Fazlur Rahman expresses it, the Qur'an is

> no treatise about God and His nature: His existence, for the Qur'an, is strictly functional—He is Creator and Sustainer of the universe and of man, and particularly the giver of guidance for man and He who judges man, indi-vidually and collectively, and metes out to him merciful justice. (1994: 1)

Consistent with Rahman's interpretation, instead of prophecy and the afterlife, I prefer to place guidance and judgment along with monotheism as the three major themes of the Qur'an. And I am also concerned with gain-ing a better understanding of the functional and pragmatic aspects of the Qur'an, both as a means of achieving a more comprehensive understanding of the foundations of Islam and as a way to improve my ability to continue reading, analyzing and interpreting the Qur'an. Consequently, while the themes of monotheism, guidance and judgment will be addressed continually throughout this book, I do not use them as the organizing criteria for the presentation of material. Rather, I base the structure of this book on my analysis of the thematic content of the fourth surah (*The Women / al-Nisa*).

The Women is a large and complex surah that contains some of the most controversial verses and ideas in the Qur'an. Because it is unlikely that most readers will have had the opportunity to carry out a close reading of the entire Qur'an, it will be instructive to use the structure and contents of one particular surah as a framework for discussing many issues of contemporary interest to Muslims and non-Muslims alike. Consequently, the present book is devoted to an exploration of the key issues addressed in the fourth surah (the themes of women, war and hypocrites).

The material is presented in four major chapters. The initial chapter on studying the Qur'an includes this brief introduction to the book, a fairly substantial description of conceptual and processual matters related to interpreting the Qur'an, a basic outline of shariah and an explication of the structure and content of the fourth surah. The remaining three chapters are thematic in nature and can be read in any order after this first chapter. As mentioned above, the headings for these three chapters are based on my analysis of the thematic structure of the fourth surah; the scriptural passages explored in this book are drawn from several places throughout the Qur'an.

The chapter on women contains discussions on the topics of marriage, lewdness, wife beating and hijab. As you might expect, the subject of marriage includes divorce, as well as an articulation of some of the rights and obligations of husbands and wives. Lewdness covers a range of sexual indiscretions including adultery, fornication and same-sex physical intimacy. The discussion of wife beating, which among other things demonstrates just how much attention a single verse of the Qur'an can garner, receives more extensive coverage than any other topic in this book. Finally, an exploration of the highly publicized matter of hijab provides insight into the social role and perception of overt displays of religious affiliation.

The chapter on war covers the topics of killing, battle, jihad and terrorism. The discussion of killing includes the act of murder, whether of a Muslim or a non-Muslim, as well as an examination of the associated recompense or punishment. The subject of battle refers primarily to armed conflict in a time of war. Jihad can refer to the struggle of the individual to remain faithful to God and it can also refer to the struggle to hold together the community of those devoted to God, including defending the community against those who would destroy it. The subject of terrorism is not addressed directly in the Qur'an, but consistent with the other issues discussed in this chapter, introducing it here provides a framework for an examination of the contemporary phenomena of suicide bombing and the use of the Qur'an to justify violence.

The chapter on hypocrites includes the topics of the believers, the People of the Book, idolatry, intoxication and the crucifixion of Jesus. In order to provide an adequate context for understanding the notion of hypocrisy, the discussion of the believers contains an examination of the five pillars of Islam as well as other essential aspects of Islamic belief and practice. The expression "People of the Book" is used primarily to refer to the scriptural linkage between the Jews, Christians and Muslims. The subject of idolatry covers an important element of the religious beliefs and traditions of pre-Islamic Arabs, but it also provides a context within which to discuss the controversial matter of depicting human figures in visual art. The subject of intoxication, which is mentioned in a few verses throughout the Qur'an, provides an excellent opportunity to demonstrate not only how the Qur'an operates as its own commentary, but also how the process of abrogation (substitution/replacement) is applied in the interpretation of the Qur'an and more broadly in Islamic jurisprudence. Further, the discussion on intoxication allows for an introduction to some aspects of Islamic responses to Sufism, music and dancing. The subject of the crucifixion of Jesus, mentioned only in the fourth surah, provides a mechanism to highlight the theme of monotheism and to illustrate the way in which the Qur'an deals with God's prophets.

EXTENSIVE knowledge of the Qur'an is not a prerequisite for reading this book. Some familiarity with the style and content of the Qur'an, gained through even a cursory reading of one of the many available English translations however, would be helpful. Of particular benefit of course, given the structure of this book, would be some time spent in reading through the fourth surah. With respect to translations, my personal preference is for the version by Muhammad Abdel Haleem (2005), who to my mind best manages to balance the seemingly contradictory demands of showing the greatest possible respect for the Qur'an as scripture while at the same time providing contemporary English readers, Muslim and non-Muslim, with a sophisticated and yet highly readable text. Among the other available translations, it is often remarked that scholars prefer that of Arthur Arberry (1996), while the one by Abdullah Yusuf Ali (2004) is extremely useful because of its extensive footnotes. From a more aesthetic perspective, the versions by Thomas Cleary (2004) and Alan Jones (2007) are interesting because of the translators' efforts to render some of the aural and poetic qualities of the original Arabic into English. I suggest that you try different translations until you find one that you are comfortable reading. As you become more familiar with the style and content of the Qur'an, you may find that your preference shifts from one version to another. The important thing is to keep reading.

Similarly, it would be helpful if readers had at least some exposure to ideas associated with how the Qur'an has been and is being analyzed and interpreted. This sort of background preparation could be gained from reading my earlier book *Reading the Qur'an in English* (Campbell 2009), or from any one of the many other available introductory texts, each of which reflects, whether explicitly or not, the peculiar approach and orientation of its author. Michael Cook's very short introduction (2000), which I find interesting but unsettling, presents the reader with a rapid glimpse of several issues related to the Qur'an, in the form of a series of unresolved and potentially unresolvable problems. Ingrid Mattson (2008) does a superior job of presenting the Qur'an as a sacred object, and of demonstrating its place in the everyday life of Muslims. The introductory texts by Neal Robinson (2003a) and Abdullah Saeed (2008a) are somewhat more technical in nature, with a greater reliance on prior knowledge of the Qur'an and of Arabic language and linguistics. Walter Wagner (2008) provides a fairly comprehensive overview of the history, content, interpretation and contemporary application of the Qur'an, in the form of a university textbook primarily designed for students at Christian seminaries.

One thought-provoking volume, written specifically for those engaged in efforts to convert Muslims, offers a short précis of every surah of the Qur'an, indicating biblical parallels and providing instructions on how to get Muslims to see the truth and come to Christianity (Ghattas and Ghattas 2009). I mention it here strictly to illustrate the palpable fear that exists in some sectors of society with respect to reading the Qur'an. The authors warn:

> If you believe the Lord is leading you to reach Muslims by gaining insight into their book, we do not want you to be naive about what you will face. For every hour spent in the Qur'an, spend another two or more in the Bible and in prayer in order to remain strong against the attacks of the Evil One. (2009: 14)

Finally, here are some practical considerations to keep in mind as you read through this book. Unless otherwise specified, when I cite passages from the Qur'an, they are taken from the translation of Abdel Haleem (2005). I refer to the individual chapters (major sections) of the Qur'an as surahs and the constituent signs (*ayahs*) as verses. Transliterations of Arabic words are given in italics, except in the cases of the words hadith, hijab, jihad, shariah, sunnah and surah, which have made their way into common parlance or are used often enough that they no longer appear foreign. I have also simplified the transliterations by eliminating diacritical marks. When I specify dates, they are expressed as common era (CE), rather than following Islamic convention as year of *hijra* (AH). The bibliography is quite extensive, especially with regard to the excellent articles contained in the *Encyclopedia of the Qur'an* (McAuliffe 2001-2006), allowing readers to follow up on items of personal interest. The subject index is designed to help readers link related discussions throughout this book as well as provide a convenient means for future reference.

※   ※

Studying the Qur'an

The primary objective of this section is to describe what it means to interpret the Qur'an and to outline how the process of interpretation has been, is being and could be carried out. As might be expected, these discussions necessarily involve the introduction of a number of technical terms from Arabic, as well as a review of concepts from such fields as philosophical hermeneutics, biblical exegesis and contemporary literary criticism. While my intention throughout this section is to clarify rather than to obscure the matter of interpretation, it is often the case that the path to genuine understanding requires navigating through a great deal of complexity. With that in mind, it is important to recognize that specialized technical vocabularies and schemas, which an outsider might reasonably view to be essential and scientifically established tools of the trade, just as often provide a convenient mechanism for professional gatekeeping and for obscuring internal disagreements over the legitimacy of methods or findings. One of the positions that I maintain throughout this book is that the task of interpreting the Qur'an should be open to anyone with the desire and energy to engage in the process, but more immediately I would suggest that there is a need to become familiar with some of the complexities that have characterized that process, in order to assess the extent to which they should inform your own reading. I begin with an overview of the structural characteristics of the Qur'an.

THE QUR'AN is composed of 114 surahs (enclosures), which, after the first short surah (*The Opening*), are arranged in decreasing order of length. One way to gain an appreciation of the variation in length of the surahs is to consider that, primarily as a means of facilitating recitation during the month of Ramadan, the Qur'an is divided into thirty sections (*ajza*, s. *juz*) of approximately equal length. In this form, surah 2 (*The Cow*) is recited over the first two days of the month, as well as on the first third of the third day, and thus constitutes about eight percent of the total length of the Qur'an. By contrast, the thirtieth *juz* is comprised of the final thirty-seven surahs (78 through 114), many of which take only about one minute to recite.

Irrespective of one's position on whether the ordering of surahs had a divine or human origin, the processes of canonization and codification of the Qur'an were carried out under the commission of the caliph Uthman, some twenty years after the death of the Prophet (Neuwirth 2002: 245-50). The notion of canonization reflects decisions regarding the authenticity and authority of the components of the text, the order in which these components are to be recorded, as well as determinations around which textual variants are to be excluded or allowed. The process of codification refers to the placement of textual materials into a written (book) form. It is important to emphasize that, even though the memorization and recitation of the Qur'an retains a prominent place in Islam, already within a relatively short period following Muhammad's death, the need to produce a definitive reference text was recognized and resolved. Over the intervening centuries, the relative merits and significance of the oral and written versions of the Qur'an have been regularly debated, with the substance of these debates informing all aspects of Islamic piety, practice and scholarship, especially with respect to determining what it means to know the Qur'an.

There is one aspect of the ordering over which there is no disagreement; namely, that the order in which the surahs appear in the written text is not the same as the order in which they were revealed (originally produced). Several attempts to establish the chronological order of the surahs have been carried out, based on various aspects of the internal structure, style and subject matter of the text, as well as on the basis of external criteria such as biographical and historical information. At the simplest level, a distinction is made between the earlier surahs that are associated with Muhammad's time in Makkah, and the later surahs that appeared following the migration (*hijra*) to Madina (622 CE). Among the more complex and comprehensive systems of arrangement that have been developed, two deserve to be mentioned here.

The first one, which likely reflects centuries of traditional Islamic understanding of this matter, appears in the Egyptian edition of the Qur'an that was printed in the 1920s. Marking the transition from hand copied versions of the Qur'an, the Egyptian edition has become the de facto standard for print versions of the Qur'an and consequently the ordering it presents has also become somewhat of a standard. The other arrangement, which primarily reflects the efforts of non-Muslim scripture scholars and linguists, and which has gained a high degree of acceptance among Muslim and non-Muslim academics, is generally referred to eponymously as the Nöldeke-Schwally version (Robinson 2003a: 77-78).

While there is a fair bit of agreement between these alternate schemes, there is one important criterion to consider when evaluating these or any other systems. Were the surahs revealed in their completed form, or were they revealed in fragments that were later stitched together? Note carefully that this question is not posed as a critique of God's actions or the timelessness and coherence of the text. The final version of the Qur'an may be just as God intended, but that does not mean that it was initially revealed/produced that way. In attempting to establish the precise chronological order of the components of the Qur'an, our concern is with understanding how the message was revealed and how these parts are related to the events of the two decades during which Muhammad is believed to have received the Qur'an. While the details of this complex and contentious area of debate are beyond the scope of this book, the issue of the structural and thematic integrity of the individual surahs is a key factor when it comes to understanding alternate approaches to interpretation.

At a more general level, in reading the Qur'an, a reliable working assumption is that the shorter surahs are chronologically prior to the longer ones—hence the advice I gave to novice readers in my previous book that they should begin by reading the Qur'an backwards (Campbell 2009: 19). At the same time, for the purposes of this book, it is fair to expect that the fourth surah will reflect a later and more mature stage of textual development, both structurally and thematically.

The surahs are made up of individual *ayahs* (signs), which also vary in length, with some containing only a couple of words and others requiring about one hundred words in English to translate. As might be expected, for the most part, the early short surahs are composed of shorter verses than the later long surahs. At the same time, of course, the length of individual verses within a surah varies quite significantly. As I have pointed out elsewhere, drastic shifts in the length of adjacent but clearly related verses might provide important insights with respect to their appropriate interpretation (Campbell 2009: 34-35). Similarly, it is probably a mere coincidence that the single longest verse in the Qur'an (2:282), commonly known as the Debt Verse, is contained in the longest surah (*The Cow*).

The names of the surahs should not be viewed as chapter titles, but rather as mnemonic devices, or simple labels, very often referring to a particular incident, object or character mentioned within the surah. For example, surah 31 is referred to as *Luqman*, most likely because it contains the story of a wise man named Luqman, who is mentioned nowhere else in the Qur'an. As a related reflection of the seemingly arbitrary nature of the way that individual surahs are named, there are even a few surahs that have alternate titles. For example, surah 17 is known either as *The Night Journey* or *The Children of Israel*.

From a thematic perspective, the shorter earlier surahs tend to focus on single issues, particularly with respect to notions of a final judgment and life after death—concepts that were certainly not a part of pre-Islamic Arab religious tradition. As the surahs get longer and later in the period of revelation, the subject matter becomes more complex and multi-faceted, and more focused on the practical concerns of establishing and maintaining the Muslim community. The later surahs also contain more numerous and lengthy references to the scripture and traditions of the Jews and Christians.

SHIFTING more directly to the subject of interpretation, the study of both the process of interpreting a text and the principles that have been established to inform that process is referred to as hermeneutics, a word derived from the name of the ancient Greek messenger god Hermes. According to myth, Hermes brought the gift of language to humans, and it was his role to transmit the will of the gods to the mere mortals inhabiting the Earth. Keeping in mind that the concept of a text refers to the actual message, rather than the specific form in which that message is recorded or transmitted (Gracia 1995, 1996), the process of interpretation can be considered to consist of three distinct actions: articulation, explanation and translation (Palmer 1969: 12-32).

The idea of articulation can be thought of as the coming into being of a text. This process is a form of interpretation because the original message is expressed at a particular place and time, in accordance with the grammar, pronunciation, syntax, vocabulary and rhetorical conventions of a particular language community. This process also recognizes the precedence and inherent superiority of the oral expression of the text over the written form, which, because it is further constrained by the writing system (alphabet) and spelling conventions (orthography) adopted by a language community, exists as a more static representation of the text. In order to recover the text—to restore its inherent dynamism—the written form must be read, preferably out loud.

The memorization and recitation of the Qur'an continues to be a fundamental aspect of Islamic religious practice, incumbent in a limited sense on every Muslim for use in their daily prayers, and on a grander scale developed to an elaborate and highly cherished form of performance art leading to celebrity status for a select few (Nelson 2001). This practical and social emphasis on the oral text is reinforced through the theological presuppositions of the revealed nature of the Qur'an (Madigan 2004), the inimitability (unparalleled supremacy) of the Qur'an (Martin 2002; Vassalou 2002), and the sanctity and perfection of the Arabic language as the medium of the revelation (Jenssen 2001). At the same time, perhaps as a reflection of a broader global shift away from oral tradition, the Qur'an as a book has developed a reverential status associated more directly with its materiality (Madigan 2001), with Abdel Haleem observing that the written text of the Qur'an has "acquired sanctity in its very orthography" (1999: 5). As with the development of recitation into an art form, visual artists have attempted to capture some of the transcendent quality and aural beauty of the Qur'an through the art of calligraphy (Blair 2008).

The second sense of the word interpretation is perhaps the most intuitive and familiar, referring to attempts to explain a text, whether literally, metaphorically, morally or in any other fashion. The process of explanation in its various forms is more generally referred to as exegesis, implying a drawing out of meaning, and as will become clear throughout the remainder of this chapter and the rest of the book, the techniques employed to explain the Qur'an (Gätje 1996) both strongly parallel and radically diverge from those that have been used over a longer period to explain the scripture of the Jews and Christians (Gorman 2001).

Just as the articulation of a text is conditioned by language, as well as linguistic and literary conventions, the process of explanation is grounded in a recognition that a text cannot exist outside of a particular context. With respect to texts whose origins go back several centuries, the environment of production would have been conditioned by a myriad of factors such as proximity to the sea, primary foodstuffs, climate and the extent of interaction with other cultures. The socio-cultural knowledge reflected in the text would be familiar to those hearing the message at the time it was produced but, with each new generation and as broader social and cultural factors changed, the text would have to be reinterpreted in such a way as to reflect those changes. As we examine such a text today, not only do we have to recognize our contemporary socio-economic conditions related to such factors as financial instability, ethnic tensions, environmental crises and the proliferation of social media, we also have to recognize that each successive effort at interpretation will have left some trace of itself on the path to establishing the way that the text is now approached and understood. This history and content of exegesis is recorded in secondary works known as commentaries and, as we will see immediately below with respect to the Qur'an, both the process of producing these works and the works themselves are referred to as *tafsir*.

Finally, translations are interpretations because they require a literal transformation of the text from one language to another. When dealing with contemporary texts, this process requires a sophisticated understanding of both the source and target languages, as well as of their associated socio-cultural contexts. When the matter is further complicated by attempting to translate a text across a considerable span of time, the translator must develop expertise in two distinct versions of the source language—one that reflects the way the language was used at the time the text was originally produced, and one that takes account of the way the language is used now. Arabic is a vibrant modern language, with many internal ethno-cultural variations, and it is naive to assume that the ability, no matter how refined, to speak and read some version of modern Arabic provides any great insight into the Arabic of the Qur'an.

Even for those scholars who dedicate their lives to studying the language and culture of the Qur'an, because it is impossible for them to be transported back fourteen centuries to the cultural milieu of Muhammad and the fledgling Muslim community, their knowledge will always be partial and imperfect. The fallout from this realization is quite sobering. Even though the written form of the Qur'an might be exactly the same as it has been for centuries, reading it today means to be reading an Arabic translation of an Arabic text. This is the only real possibility. You cannot read the original text of the Qur'an.

With respect to hermeneutics as the theoretical framework or articulation of assumptions informing the process of interpretation, the exegesis of the Qur'an certainly reflects the socio-cultural history and intellectual heritage of the Arabs, but it equally reflects the influence of broader Semitic and Hellenistic worldviews, medieval scholasticism, renaissance humanism, Enlightenment rationalism, as well as more recent scholarly trends grounded in Marxism, existentialism, social constructionism, various forms of feminism and postmodernism (Arkoun 2001). Even recent scholarship that might be viewed as representing mainstream internalist Islamic interpretations of the Qur'an tends to reflect the influence of major thinkers associated with the development of modern biblical exegesis and philosophical hermeneutics, such as Friedrich Schleiermacher, Wilhelm Dilthey, Martin Heidegger, Hans-Georg Gadamer and Paul Ricoeur (Palmer 1969; Abou El Fadl 2001).

Returning for a moment to the mythical world of the Greeks, Hermes was charged with delivering messages to humanity, but as a means of making the job more interesting he was at liberty to decide how he would do so. Consequently, messages were often delivered in the form of a riddle, leaving the recipients to search for an answer, very often with their success in understanding the message being based on their knowledge of their own circumstances. I do not raise this issue to imply malice aforethought on the part of an intermediary in delivering the Qur'an or any other text, but rather to highlight one of the central hermeneutical problems—the inability of language to adequately capture and convey meaning. Given this environment of uncertainty in communication, there has always been a tension between the recognition of philosophical variability and the desire for theological consistency in the interpretation of God's will (Achrati 2006, 2008). In more recent times, this tension has extended to reflect the incompatibility of those worldviews embedded in a morass of ethno-cultural restrictions with those devoted to taking adequate account of contemporary social reality.

Ingrid Mattson makes the excellent point that in the early years of Islam, exegesis preceded hermeneutics (2008: 176). In other words, the regular interpretation of the Qur'an and the application of particular verses to the settlement of political, religious and social issues was carried out prior to the establishment of any consistent methodology or interpretive principles being developed, codified, distributed and shared among religious authorities. Accepting the vagaries of human nature, in any given circumstance, it is likely that interpretations were motivated as much by political, economic and emotional conditions as they were by rational and reasoned factors. Even though we might grant that in recognition of these inconsistencies scholars eventually set out to establish interpretive criteria that met the highest standards of theological and scientific rigor, it is not unreasonable to speculate that many of the rules and procedures that were established were done retrospectively, either to justify or discredit what had already taken place.

As mentioned above, while the word *tafsir* is commonly used to refer to the formal commentaries written on the Qur'an, it is also used to describe the processes of interpretation that inform these works. When used in this latter processual sense, a further critical, and yet not uniformly applied, distinction is usually made between the notion of *tafsir* and the associated idea of *tawil*. Claude Gilliot suggests that while *tafsir* is quite commonly used to mean an explanation, *tawil* refers to the original meaning of the text (2002: 100). He goes on to relate that Ibn Abbas (d. 688) is credited with having stated that when it comes to understanding the Qur'an, there is the literal meaning (*tafsir*) that the scholars know and the deeper meaning (*tawil*) that only God knows. Mohammad Kamali suggests that *tafsir* is the process whereby a meaning is deduced directly from the given words and sentences, while *tawil* goes beyond the literal level to get at the hidden meaning that can only be accessed through speculative reasoning and independent (personal) thought (2003: 119). The critical point for present purposes is that this distinction demonstrates that, from the earliest period, Muslim scholars openly acknowledged the existence of multiple layers of meaning within the text, not all of which are equally accessible to the reader. By extension, it is not unreasonable to suggest that, in spite of primacy of place given to the Qur'an, a full understanding of the text is not discernible from the text itself.

Gilliot divides the historical development of pre-modern (classical and medieval) exegesis of the Qur'an into three periods, roughly corresponding to initiatives originating in the 1st, 2nd and 3rd centuries after the death of Muhammad, with the final period lasting several hundred years (2002: 104-10). The works of the first formative period are categorized as being paraphrastic, narrative or legal in content. While the first of these types simply consisted of paraphrases or restatements of the text, the mere existence of such works suggests that the Arabic of the Qur'an was adequately different from what native speakers were accustomed to, even only a few decades removed from the text's origins, so as to require some level of clarification. The second type focused less on the actual text, and was devoted instead to elaborating on the context of the Qur'an, through the telling of stories drawn from Byzantine, Egyptian and Persian folklore, but especially reflecting the traditional myths and legends of the Jews and Christians. The early legal commentaries basically amounted to rearrangements of the text, in order to bring together all of the verses dealing with almsgiving, marriage, usury and other matters that would arise in the social administration of the Muslim community.

The second period, referred to as the intermediary and decisive stage, is characterized by a more systematic and formalized approach to the text based on developments in Arabic grammar and linguistics. While placing exegesis on a more secure scholarly footing, at least initially, the techniques appear to have been used less for explaining the text and more for demonstrating its miraculous character. A number of scholars rejected grammatical approaches because they thought that these efforts served to reduce the text to a mere construct of letters and words, and because they associated proper exegetical technique with the use of hadith and biographical materials.

Gilliot's third period, which he refers to as the constitutive Sunni phase, reflects what might be viewed as the era of establishment of an orthodox corpus of commentaries based on traditional authority, as documented in chains of transmission that codified an intellectual lineage back to the Prophet, through his companions, successors and the generations of intermediary scholars and teachers. The defining work in this genre is associated with al-Tabari (d. 923), who recorded 13,026 chains with respect to some 35,400 cases of interpretation (Gilliot 2002: 111). These works, which tended to be quite long, examined each verse in order, compiling the various scholarly opinions about the complete spectrum of interpretive matters arising in the verse, and then providing the respective lineage of authority associated with each scholarly opinion. Among other key commentators associated with this period are: Ibn Taymiyya (d. 1328), Ibn Kathir (d. 1373), whose work is readily available in English translation, and al-Suyuti (d. 1505).

Parallel with the development of these more inclusive commentaries, a variety of specialized works that were legal, philosophical, sectarian or mystical in orientation were also being produced in this period. In some cases the legal commentaries dealt only with the interpretation of the specifically legal verses from the Qur'an, while in other instances the entire text was interpreted from a legal perspective. Those works that were influenced by developments in speculative theology reflected arguments about such matters as the meaning of free will and the extent to which personal opinion could be considered a valid basis for interpretation. There were also a number of sectarian commentaries produced by groups such as the Kharijis and Zaydis, but perhaps of greater historical significance were the ones associated with the Imami Shia. Mystical interpretations were largely introspective in nature, reflecting an integration of Sufi religious practice and philosophy with Sunni mystical doctrine on subjects like the isolated letters, the divine names and the *basmalah*. Key individuals associated with this approach are: al-Tustari (d. 896), al-Sulami (d. 1021), Ibn al-Arabi (d. 1240) and the Ottoman al-Brusawi (d. 1725), who made extensive use of Persian mystical poetry in his commentaries.

With respect to more modern commentaries (from roughly the last 150 years), Rotraud Wielandt observes that while many scholars continued to work in the classical tradition without making substantially new contributions to our understanding, some innovative trends have emerged, primarily in Egypt (2002: 124). He suggests that these new efforts reflect attempts to reconcile the text of the Qur'an with the findings of modern science and the need to determine the make-up of an appropriate political and social order for Islamic nations that either paves the way for assimilation with the dominant American and European worldviews, or provides a plausible alternative. With respect to the actual process of constructing commentaries, Wielandt points out that the traditional pattern of verse-by-verse analysis that strictly follows the verse order of the text is giving way to more thematically based approaches, in which clusters of related verses are discussed together (2002: 125). He identifies six distinct innovative trends.

The first trend is represented by the independent work of Sayyid Ahmad Khan (d. 1898) in India and Muhammad Abduh (d. 1905) in Egypt, and entails the interpretation of the Qur'an from the perspective of Enlightenment rationalism. The principle idea informing this approach is that revealed religion should not be beyond the grasp of, or inconsistent with, the human capacity for understanding. The second trend is referred to as scientific exegesis, and is based on the assumption that the findings of modern science have already been anticipated in the text of the Qur'an. Among the proponents of this approach, the majority of whom were trained in medicine or the natural sciences rather than theology, the most prominent is Shaykh Tantawi Jawhari (d. 1940), but in Europe and North America this approach is more commonly associated with the writings of Maurice Bucaille (2003). The third trend involves interpreting the Qur'an from the perspective of literary studies, treating the Qur'an as the ultimate expression of Arabic literature, and thus exposing it to the same sort of analytical scrutiny applied to the Bible, or the works of Homer and Shakespeare. This initiative is associated with the teachings of Amin al-Khuli (d. 1967), and with the efforts of his students, including his wife Aisha Abd al-Rahman (pen name Bint al-Shati, d. 1999), to carry out such a program. As Wielandt points out, this approach was condemned by the religious scholars at al-Azhar, to the extent that a memorandum was released in which Muhammad Ahmad Khalaf Allah was declared a criminal for having suggested in his doctoral thesis that some of the narratives in the Qur'an were not historically true (Wielandt 2002: 134).

The fourth new approach is predicated on the notion of taking full account of the historicity (evidential place-ment in history) of the Qur'an, in an effort to resolve the hermeneutic tension between the Qur'an as an eternal and universal message and as a concrete text that originated in a specific place and time. One of the key advocates of this ap-proach, Fazlur Rahman (d. 1988), suggested that scholars need to follow a three-step process whereby they first try to understand a particular pronouncement in its original context, then identify and separate out the core meaning or lesson, and finally apply this insight in the present. A more scientifically rigorous version of this approach was developed by Nasr Hamid Abu Zayd (b. 1943), who incor-porated ideas from information theorist Claude Shannon, and declared that in the case of the Qur'an, as with any other text: "The information contained in a message can be understand only if the sender transmits it in a code (i.e., a system of signs) known to the recipient" (Wielandt 2002: 136). A third major figure in this area is Mohammad Arkoun (b. 1928), who emphasizes the performative aspect of the oral Qur'an across history, and who looks to developments in historical semiotics and sociolinguistics to gain a more comprehensive and relevant understanding of the text.

Sayyid Qutb (d. 1966) was one of the principle advocates of the fifth approach, which, in stark contrast to the other innovations discussed by Wielandt, is characterized by a call for Muslims to return to the practice of Islam as it was carried out in the time of the Prophet. According to this perspective, because the Qur'an is viewed as contemporary for any age, the task is not to understand its meaning on the basis of the challenges facing modern society, but rather to alter the way we live today so that it is consistent with the way that the Prophet and his immediate companions lived in accordance with God's will. One of the criticisms levelled against this approach is that Qutb and others place too heavy a reliance on the hadith literature as a means of accessing what they consider to be the original and ideal form of Islamic practice. Similar issues emerge in the discussion of Islamism further below in the introduction to the chapter on war.

Finally, thematic approaches are described as a means of avoiding the biases related with the selective interpretation of isolated verses, by approaching the text through the lens of a few organizing themes. In this manner, it is argued, a more comprehensive and balanced understanding of the content and intent of the text can be developed. By extension, thematic analyses are seen as a better preparation for the practical use of the Qur'an in sermons, lessons and pubic addresses. From the perspective of the interpreter, the thematic approach allows commentators to ask questions of the text as a whole and to develop explanations based on their own particular interests. Wielandt ends his survey by looking at the controversial work of Egyptian philosopher Hasan Hanafi (b. 1935), who, in advocating a revolutionary thematic approach to interpreting the Qur'an, suggests that the text has no significance of its own, only gaining meaning to the extent that it is drawn upon by the interpreter to support his or her socio-political commitment.

※

HAVING briefly reviewed some important developments in the history of the interpretation of the Qur'an, the final part of this section is devoted to an exploration of an interpretive framework outlined by Abdullah Saeed (2006, 2008b). In contrast to the more conservative textualist and semi-textualist approaches advocated by many commentators, Saeed suggests that some scholars are beginning to take what he calls a contextualist approach to the Qur'an that starts from a position of "questioning accepted practices and methods of thought within Islamic tradition" and is aligned with an emphasis on "social justice, human rights and interfaith relations" (2008b: 222). The four stages in the contextualist approach are referred to as encounter, critical analysis, meaning for the first recipients and meaning for the present (2006: 149-54, 2008b: 226-27).

Encountering the Qur'an means to become familiar with the text through both reading and listening. Right from the outset we are confronted with the problem of language, with the majority of Muslim and non-Muslim scholars agreeing with Mustansir Mir, who suggests that with respect to the interpretive process: "The foremost requirement, of course, is possession of a thorough knowledge of the language of the Qur'an, and this requirement is fulfilled through a close and careful study of the language of the time at which the Qur'an was revealed" (2008: 7). As I have already suggested, I am not an advocate of this position, partially because I do not think that it is an attainable goal, and partially because it is has been used in a protectionist manner to exclude and prohibit large numbers from participation in the interpretive process. Certainly, if your objective is to study the early development of the Arabic language, as reflected in and influenced by the Qur'an, then the intensive study of the relevant ancient languages (not just Arabic) is paramount. However, if your intention is to gain an appreciation of the content of the Qur'an, then you should read the text in a language that you understand.

At the same time, I think there is much to be gained from listening to the Qur'an being recited in Arabic. For one thing, it provides outsiders (those with little or no knowledge of Arabic) with an appreciation of the way in which the vast majority of Muslims encounter the text on a daily basis. And there is an additional benefit. As Michael Sells effectively demonstrates with respect to the early surahs that deal primarily with eschatological matters, the phrasing, rhyme schemes and word choice used in these short surahs create a sense of urgency and excitement that transmits much of the message of the verses even to those who do not literally understand what is being said (1999). By extension, through listening to excerpts from various locations throughout the Qur'an, the listener can gain some appreciation of the linguistic and thematic complexities, phrasing patterns and vocal tone embedded in the structure of the text.

Reading the Qur'an in any language can be quite confusing. Kate Zebiri explains that unlike the Bible, which is composed of the works of multiple authors, contains large tracts of narrative, and is for the most part chronological, the Qur'an is more of a mosaic "containing many elements which are continually juxtaposed in slightly different ways to other elements, with a strong element of repetition" (2003: 109). Consequently, rather than trying to read the Qur'an from cover to cover, whether front to back, or back to front, it makes just as much if not more sense simply to flip the book open to any page and start reading, flipping to another spot whenever too much confusion emerges or you start to lose interest. I see absolutely no benefit in ever reading the Qur'an from the so-called beginning to the end—in fact I would suggest that the very concepts of beginning and end apply to the Qur'an in only a limited manner.

Another potential stumbling block when setting out to read the Qur'an is determining which of the many available translations to select. When it comes to English translations, two particular issues emerge. First, there are still significant differences between British and American usage, and, even though my personal preference is for a British version of the Qur'an (Abdel Haleem 2005), I think that this translation comes closest to reflecting, if such a thing exists, contemporary global English usage. By contrast, as demonstrated in the following verse from the Jones (2007) translation: "We shall call on the myrmidons of Hell" (96:18), other British translations appear to assume a particular educational background among readers. Especially with respect to attracting a larger and broader readership, I am not sure that a working knowledge of Homer's *Iliad* should be considered a prerequisite for delving into the Qur'an. The second problem, which primarily applies to older translations, is what appears to be a deliberate attempt to mimic the King James version of the Bible by employing an archaic form of language, as if the liberal use of thee, thou and whilst will somehow give the translation greater authority and a more sacred look. As previously stated, readers should sample a couple of different translations before venturing too far into the text.

As one final point before moving on to the next step, this process of encountering the Qur'an can be viewed as a pre-interpretive stage, aimed at providing the reader with a surface level exposure to the text in a purely objective sense, as a collection of words and phrases put together in a particular way. This is, in fact, an important step to take. When young Muslims set out to memorize the entire Qur'an, their focus is on proper pronunciation and recitation technique. Their ability, or even their desire, to understand what they are reciting is a secondary and unnecessary part of their learning, reserved primarily for those who will go on to the formal study of Islamic theology and law. For those who are reading the Qur'an in a language they understand, however difficult a task it might prove to be, their initial goal should be to take the time to encounter the text before engaging in the interpretive process or passing judgment on what the text is saying.

The second step of the contextualist approach is to analyze the text independent of its historical or contemporary context. It is at this stage where issues of structure, grammar, syntax, literary context and literary form are taken into account, and it is at this stage that it would appear most critical to possess a sophisticated understanding of Arabic language and linguistics. I will concede this point if it is your intention to carry out your own translation of the Qur'an, but I am entirely convinced that there is just as much, if not more, that can be learned at this stage by applying techniques associated more generally with literary criticism. The Qur'an makes extensive use of repetition, parallelism, chiasmus, chaining, concatenation and other devices, as will be demonstrated continually throughout the remainder of the book, that are not lost in translation, and that are common to all literatures (Mir 1988). Given doctrinal statements about the inimitability of the Qur'an and the religiously conservative view that the word of God cannot be subjected to the same scrutiny as the word of human authors, it is important to remember that these are statements of faith that, in my view, should not be interpreted as prohibitions against the study of the Qur'an as text. Similarly, it is important to ensure that deliberations at this stage of analysis do not draw upon elements from the third stage of analysis—the critical point being the difference between co-text and context, with the former referring to the surrounding text and the latter to surrounding events (Abdul-Raof 2003). In other words, at this stage, the process of interpretation should be internal to the text.

One of the best examples of the complexity of Arabic usage in the Qur'an, which might easily be viewed as an excellent justification for learning a great deal of Arabic prior to studying the Qur'an, is with respect to a rhetorical device known as *iltifat*, which literally means to turn aside or shift attention toward (Abdel Haleem 1999: 184-

210; Robinson 2003a: 224-55). Abdel Haleem explains that *iltifat* is of six types: change in person (first, second and third), number (singular, dual and plural), addressee, tense of the verb, case marker or the substitution of a noun for a pronoun (Abdel Haleem 1999: 188). Whatever the intended use of these literary manipulations might have been, the practical effect in many instances is to leave the reader wondering who is speaking, or who is being spoken to or of, in any particular verse. As will be demonstrated in the discussion of the Beating Verse (4:34) in the next chapter, as an aid to readers, translators will often indicate which person, number or addressee is intended in a particular instance by using superscripts, footnotes or parenthetical additions to the text. Irrespective of these aids, however, I remain unconvinced that those with an extensive knowledge of Arabic are any less confused about the proper interpretation of certain verses in the Qur'an than those without it.

Similarly, knowledge of Arabic might be seen as essential when it comes to translating or further interpreting words that have more than one meaning (polysemy). In these instances, readers must rely on other clues, such as the co-text, to determine how a particular word should be understand in one instance, and perhaps completely differently in another (Berg 2004). Not only is polysemy a challenge, there are a number of words in the Qur'an that are not of Arabic origin (Rippin 2002). These loanwords, from languages such as Ethiopic, Greek, Hebrew, Persian and Syriac, might have been integrated into the Arabic language prior to the production of the Qur'an, and certainly all language communities borrow words as the result of trade or conquest.

Irrespective of concerns with regard to what language the Qur'an was written in, or is read in, as the following verse demonstrates, there is a certain self-awareness, or re-flexivity, within the text itself that warns of the inability of any language to adequately express meaning:

It is He who sent this Scripture down to you [Prophet]. Some of its verses are definite in meaning—these are the cornerstone of the Scripture—and others are ambiguous. The perverse at heart eagerly pursue the ambiguities in their attempt to make trouble and to pin down a specific meaning of their own; only God knows the true meaning. Those firmly grounded in knowledge say, "We believe in it; it is all from our Lord"—only those with real perception will take heed. (3:7)

Leah Kinberg outlines the various ways in which the problem of the ambiguous verses has been handled (2001). Some commentators have argued that only God knows the meaning of these verses, and that they are not to be interpreted because this would somehow imply, in direct contradiction of the doctrine of inimitability, that the Qur'an was imperfect and in need of clarification.

Similarly, some scholars have suggested that interpretation could lead to dissension among the faithful, as happened when the Mutazilis interpreted certain verses (18:29, 76:30) as supporting their doctrine of free will, in opposition to the orthodox Sunni position on predestination. In contrast, others have suggested that the ambiguous verses are to be interpreted against the background of the clear verses and the Qur'an as a whole. Part of the argument in support of this position is based on the idea that if the meaning of all verses was clear then there would be no need for interpretation and thus there would be no difference between the learned and the ignorant. In this view ambiguity serves as a stimulus for people to develop in religious knowledge, leading to potentially greater rewards in the world to come.

At the same time, various Muslim scholars throughout the ages have suggested that the Qur'an is its own best commentary. For example, Ibn Taymiyya (d. 1328) indicated: "What is given in a general way in one place is explained in detail in another place. What is given briefly in one place is expanded in another" (Abdel Haleem 1999: 160). In some instances, this position has been interpreted to mean that no information from outside the Qur'an is necessary, or potentially even relevant, for understanding the meaning of the text. In other cases, it has facilitated what is often referred to as an atomistic approach to interpreting the Qur'an, whereby individual verses are interpreted in isolation from the verses around them, even though they might be compared to verses from elsewhere in the Qur'an that cover the same or similar subject matter.

Abdel Haleem uses the example of the interpretation of surah 57 (*Iron/al-Hadid*) to demonstrate how two prominent Arabic scholars and translators of the Qur'an, Richard Bell and Alan Jones, missed the opportunity to develop a more comprehensive and holistic understanding of the surah, because their analyses of this surah were based on the assumption that surahs "comprise a conglomeration of essentially disparate material, and jump from one theme to another in a disjointed, haphazard manner" (Abdel Haleem

2008: 128). Intertextuality—verses from various locations in the Qur'an that address similar issues—can be a useful aid to interpretation, but so can a close examination of the verses immediately preceding and following a particular verse or passage of interest—the co-text.

The third step in the contextualist approach is to establish the meaning of the Qur'an for those who heard it first. In recognition of the fact that language use is situated in particular times and places, Saeed observes that, "the Qur'an adopted culturally specific symbols, metaphors and expressions in order to convey its message more easily to its first recipients" (2008b: 228). As a means of gaining insight into Arabic culture at the time the early Islamic community was developing, commentators have relied heavily on the sunnah, as documented in *sira* (Raven 2006) and hadith (Juynboll 2002).

The concept of sunnah refers most specifically to the life example of Muhammad, and in a more general sense to the notion of tradition, as established by the Prophet and his companions and immediate successors (Afsaruddin 2008). One source of this tradition is the biographies (*sira*) of the Prophet, of which the oldest and most authoritative is attributed to Ibn Ishaq (d. 767), which we possess in a version edited by Ibn Hisham (d. 834) that is available in an English translation by Alfred Guillaume (Ibn Hisham 1955).

There are several good modern biographies of Muhammad, such as those by Karen Armstrong (1991), Martin Lings (1983), Tariq Ramadan (2007) and Maxime Rodinson (1980), which reflect a variety of perspectives, but which also continue to demonstrate the importance of the life of the Prophet in developing a proper understanding of Islam and in learning to live as a Muslim in the world. Among other things, the biographical material provides information about the circumstances of revelation, establishing a context within which to explain why certain verses were revealed, who they might be referring to, and how they should be understood (Rippin 2003).

The concept of hadith refers to collections of the sayings and practices of Muhammad, that reflect his efforts to understand and apply the message that was being revealed to him and to teach others to do so as well (Brown 2009). A hadith consists of the actual text of the tradition (*matn*), which is preceded by the listing of a chain of transmission (*isnad*), linking the tradition back to the Prophet. Within a few centuries after Muhammad's death, because the number of hadith had multiplied so greatly, certain scholars set out to verify the authenticity of the various traditions through systematic and exhaustive analysis of the chains of transmission. As a result of these efforts, six canonical Sunni hadith collections were established, of which those by Muhammad b. Ismail al-Bukhari (d. 870) and Muslim b. al-Hajjaj (d. 875) have become the most dominant. Among the Shia, the hadith collections of al-Kulayni (d. 939) and al-Majlisi (d. 1700) are especially important with respect to the interpretation of the Qur'an. The content of the hadith literature covers a broad range of topics, but with particular reference to the Qur'an, details are provided on how the various fragments were brought together, what variations in the text were permitted, the proper recitation of the text, instructions as to appropriate methods of interpretation, historical details on the occasions of revelation and reflections on the special significance of certain surahs and verses.

Even though the hadith literature is considered second only to the Qur'an, in terms of authority in Islam, there is widespread recognition that this literature has been subject to deliberate forgery and unintentional fabrication (Kamali 2003: 87-92). For example, certain hadith, such as "eggplants are the cure for every illness," were fabricated by heretical groups within Islam, in an effort to discredit the importance of tradition. Certain European scholars, such as Ignaz Goldziher (1981) and Joseph Schacht (1964), who viewed Islam as a manufactured religion, and who modelled their analyses of the Qur'an and early Islamic literature on advances in biblical studies, raised serious questions about the authenticity and historicity of the hadith literature. Among Muslim critics, Syed Ahmed Khan (d. 1898) was of the opinion that hadith were not legally binding on Muslims, and the Malaysian Kassim Ahmad even goes so far as to suggest that the hadith literature is anti-Islamic (1997).

The final step of the contextualist approach is to determine the meaning for the present, which requires an examination of the current context in which a particular section of the Qur'an is being applied, or may be applicable. I stressed before that we cannot go back to the early years of Islam and it is impossible for me to read the Qur'an outside of my present context, one that is conditioned by any number of political, social and cultural events that have a direct link to Islam: the September 11, 2001, destruction of the World Trade Center, global paranoia over jihadi terrorist sleeper cells, the ongoing and seemingly endless wars in Afghanistan, Iraq and elsewhere, the perpetually unresolved Palestinian question and broader concerns, variously described, with the growth of Muslim populations in several European countries, as well as in the United States and Canada. Along with these uncertainties, many of the established parameters with respect to theories of translation and interpretive frameworks are being called in to question.

In a recent book, Ziad Elmarsafy demonstrates the political aspect of translation through an exploration of the impact of the 1734 translation by George Sale (1921) among others on the development of Western attitudes towards Islam, especially as represented in the works of Voltaire and Goethe (Elmarsafy 2009b). In a related conference paper, Elmarsafy advocates for a more collaborative approach to the translation of the Qur'an, based on the precedent set by Roman Catholic scholars who worked together to produce what came to be known as the *Jerusalem Bible* (2009a: 14). This collaborative work was initiated through an encyclical issued by Pope Pius XII, in which he encouraged Catholics to translate the Bible from the original Hebrew and Greek, rather than from older Latin translations. The project was started near the end of the Second World War and the finished translation was published in French in 1961, and in English in 1966. Of course, an even earlier precedent for this sort of undertaking can be found in the case of the Greek translation of the Hebrew Bible, known as the *Septuagint*, which was prepared in Alexandria, Egypt, between the 3rd and 1st centuries BCE by seventy-two (the name implies seventy) scholars.

Regarding the exegetical aspect of interpretation, Saeed mentions Muhammad Shahrour, a self-taught scholar of Islam originally trained as a civil engineer, who suggests that anyone, be they believers or unbelievers, Muslim or non-Muslim, Arab speakers or not, can engage in the interpretation of the Qur'an (Saeed 2008b: 235). While this position might sound somewhat anarchistic, potentially opening the doors to an entirely relativistic environment, in which no interpretation can be seen to be more accurate or more authoritative than any other, Jorge Gracia observes that:

> relational interpretations take place within established communities, and it is within these communities that the criteria for their legitimacy and value are developed. This is why, in general, relational interpretations cannot be said to be based on individual opinion. Indeed, the supervision that these communities exercise over their particular kinds of interpretations is often so strict that it discourages innovation and change to such a degree that they are sometimes brought about only at a great cost to those who do it. Interpretive communities tend to be conservative and set in their ways, and development is usually tolerated only within narrow parameters and at a slow pace. (2000: 57)

This holds true whether the interpretive communities represent orthodox Islam, Marxists, feminists or contextualists, although, in their defence, Saeed stresses that contextualists are less dogmatic and proscriptive, "seeking to promote an Islam which is pluralistic, liberating and inclusive" (2008b: 223). To the extent that Saeed's advocacy might appear a bit optimistic, even in our current context of global economics and social media, Peter Mandaville comments that:

Globalization does not in and of itself instantiate a plu-
ralization of Islamic authority insofar as there has never
existed a situated, singular source of authentic Muslim
knowledge. Rather, globalization can be seen to represent
a further shift in the extent and intensity of debate about
the meaning and nature of the authoritative in Islam.
(2007: 102)

WITH RESPECT to new approaches to the study of the
Qur'an that can be said to reflect some sort of broader social
or political concern or agenda, Kate Zebiri states that:

A rhetorical study of the Qur'an is in large measure a
study of the Qur'an's effectiveness, not just in a literary/
stylistic sense but also in a psychological sense, which
is not an area with which Western scholarship has been
particularly concerned in the past. (2003: 99)

One realm in which the psychological effectiveness of
the Qur'an is perhaps most evident is with respect to the
development, and ongoing justification, of Islamic attitudes
towards women. Over the past decade or so, rhetorical
studies of the Qur'an have been carried out by women, especially those with faculty positions in European and North
American universities, in part to determine if in fact the
Qur'an provides a firm basis for the way in which Muslim
women are treated in various parts of the world, and in
part to claim, or reclaim, a position for women as legitimate interpreters of the Qur'an.

Juliane Hammer surveys the interpretative efforts of three American Muslim women, Amina Wadud, Asma Barlas and Nimat Barazangi, who, following the example of Leila Ahmed (1992), advocate for an "ethical, gender-just Islam," and who argue that interpretive efforts must be linked to social activism (Hammer 2008). For these women, who received their graduate education in the United States, their identity as Muslims and as women is foundational to their analysis. Wadud, who converted to Islam as a student at university, began her intensive study of the Qur'an with the premise that if she found that the text portrayed women as inferior to men, she would leave Islam. Not only did she discover that the Qur'an presented men and women as equal in all ways, she also became a harsh critic of the hegemony of Arabic language training as the gateway to studying the Qur'an, stating that "it is unfathomable that the Lord of all worlds is not potentially multilingual" (qtd. in Hammer 2008: 452). Her activism, which includes leading mixed gender congregational prayers, has drawn extensive media coverage and criticism. Barlas, who was born and raised in Pakistan, works primarily within the academy, challenging the perception that Islam is patriarchal. She joins Wadud in questioning the centrality of Arabic to the study of Islam, concluding that "if we can read the Qur'an in translation, we can also interpret it in translation" (qtd. in Hammer 2008: 452). Barazangi, originally from Syria, centers her activities less directly on Islamic studies and more on issues pertaining to women's education, both with respect to access and form. Her scholarship is firmly rooted in the position that "every individual Muslim, man or woman, has not only the authority but also the responsibility to read and interpret the Qur'an for him or herself" (Hammer 2008: 450).

Hammer goes on explain that the assessment of the agendas of these three women by other religion scholars is quite mixed. For example, Jose Ignacio Cabezon suggests that while identity as a woman or a Muslim might influence the selection of research agendas, this identity in no way privileges or authorizes the findings of any researcher (2004). Darlene Juschka, who attributes little value to faith-based research, sees the efforts of Wadud, Barlas and Barazangi as naive, because it is impossible to strip the Qur'an, and Islam more generally, of its history, both with respect to its origins and to how it has been understood for the last fourteen centuries (Juschka 2001). In contrast to these positions, Gisela Webb advocates for more identity-centred research, as she expresses in the title of the introduction to her book on North American Muslim women scholar-activists "May Muslim women speak for themselves, please" (2000), arguing that these women have no "choice but to translate their findings into actions aimed at change in their societies and communities" (Hammer 2008: 456).

While I stated at the beginning of this section that my intention was to clarify the subject of interpretation rather than contribute to further confusion, I trust that readers now have a greater appreciation not only for the complexities of the interpretive process but for the necessity to continue developing and applying new approaches and techniques.

Shariah

Ziauddin Sardar states that shariah is "the core of the world-view of Islam" (2003: 64), and Khaled Abou El Fadl maintains that by the 8th century shariah had emerged as the de facto successor to the authority that had once resided with the Qur'an and God's Messenger (2001: 12). However, in spite of its central importance in the evolution and contemporary practice of Islam, the concept of shariah is still greatly misunderstood. Literally meaning the way to the water source, Sardar suggests that anything worthy of being called an Islamic civilization would be one in which the values of shariah had attained their highest expression (2003: 64). At present, however, our appreciation of the role of shariah and our understanding of how it is constituted and applied are overly conditioned by the self-serving misrepresentations proffered by certain minority factions within Islam and by the equally artificial constraints associated with the content and internal logic of contemporary European and American legal codes. Putting these factors aside, within the context of trying to understand how the Qur'an was and is being interpreted, I would suggest that a genuine exploration of shariah begins with the realization that it is a methodology—not a code of law.

At the same time, it is important to recognize that the contemporary practice of shariah is for the most part being carried out within the framework of formalized schools of thought that had become established by about the end of the 3nd Islamic century. Based on the writings of the prominent jurists from which they derived their names, the four Sunni schools and the regions in which they are presently predominant are the Hanafi in the Indian subcontinent, the Maliki in North and West Africa, the Shafi'i in Malaysia and

Indonesia and the Hanbali in Arabia, with the Shia Jafari school dominating in Iran and Iraq. As Sardar observes, this division into separate and distinct legal schools was never meant to be rigid and restrictive on later developments; rather, it was reflective of the political and philosophical circumstances at the time in which they were established (2003: 66). Nor were the judgments passed by the jurists associated with these schools meant to be final and pro-scriptive at the time they were presented, or for all time, as illustrated in the following aphorism usually attributed to Abu Hanifa: "Our school is correct, but may be wrong; the school of those who disagree with us is wrong, but it may be right" (Mattson 2008: 207). Given the general human resistance to change and the fact that generations of jurists have been trained within this institutional framework, it is easy to understand why Muslims and non-Muslims alike might tend to equate shariah with sets of laws.

Viewing it as the primary means through which Muslims maintain the internal stability of their communities as they adapt to change, Sardar suggests that shariah represents an "infinite spiritual and worldly thirst that is never satisfied" (2003: 64). The allusion to water is quite appropriate, evoking some of the imagery of the Qur'an and calling to mind the oft-cited aphorism of a pre-Socratic Greek philosopher. Abdel Haleem points out that, in the Qur'an, water is always spoken about as being "lively and full of movement" (1999: 36), and Heraclitus is well known for having expressed his view that change is the only constant in the phrase: "You can never step into the same river twice." While both of these expressions seem to suggest that there is no one interpretation for all time, they also help us to understand that a living and vibrant Islamic community must continually renegotiate the interpretive balance between the eternal guidance of the Qur'an and the persistence of change in everyday life. Abdel Haleem goes on to suggest that there are three purposes for discussions of water in the Qur'an: as proof of God's existence, as proof of God's care, and as proof of resurrection (1999: 38). I do not think that it is too much of a stretch to conclude that, from an Islamic perspective, these three purposes explain the need for the continued development and application of shariah.

As a starting point for understanding shariah in practical terms, it is necessary to recognize that, in contrast to the binary logic of many legal systems in which acts are either legal or illegal, Islamic jurisprudence allows for five categories of action:

obligatory – *wajib, fard*
encouraged/recommended – *mandub*
neutral/permitted – *mubah*
discouraged/repugnant – *makruh*
forbidden – *haram*

As might be anticipated, there are alternate Arabic terms for some of these categories, and there are a variety of ways of explaining precisely what is meant by each of them, and which particular actions fall into one category or another. For example, jurists of the Hanafi school insist that a distinction must be made between the concepts of *wajib* and *fard*, when it comes to understanding the meaning of obligatory, with *fard* implying a legal norm arrived at through certain evidence, and *wajib* implying a legal norm determined by probable evidence (Hallaq 1997: 40). In either case, once it is determined that a particular action is obligatory, then punishment is associated with the omission of that act. Praying five times a day is obligatory for all Muslims, but, even though an individual might be chastised or berated by family members or the community for not carrying out this obligation, the punishment in this case will come on the Day of Judgment.

With respect to those things that are encouraged, a person is rewarded for their performance, but is not punished for not performing them. Examples of this meritorious sort of action include fasting outside of Ramadan, performing extra cycles of prayer and giving more than the required amount to charity. Neutral matters carry with them neither reward nor punishment, and thus are entirely discretionary. This category covers a broad range of seemingly mundane and quotidian activities, such as choice of occupation, preferring to sleep on your back or your side, or having scrambled eggs for breakfast. Discouraged acts are rewarded when omitted and punished when committed. Insolence, arrogance, drawing a conclusion without adequate evidence, cheating in a business transaction and taking advantage of the poor or less fortunate all fall into this category. Finally, punishment is associated with commission of those acts that are forbidden, such as eating pork, committing adultery or marrying two sisters simultaneously.

While the practice of shariah is a worldly matter, ultimately, reward and punishment are in God's hands. In those cases where specific punishments are spelled out in the Qur'an or were practised by the Prophet during his lifetime, judges determine if in fact an individual has committed an offence that warrants that punishment, and it can then be carried out. In other instances, as mentioned above with respect to prayer, punishment is something that will only be meted out in the next life. Most often, legal scholars are called upon to provide guidance, by determining which category a particular action falls in to, thus helping people to ensure that they will not be condemned to the fire.

Another important concept related to these five categories is the notion of *halal*, which can be thought of as a statement about what is lawful or what constitutes a correct course of action. The most common use of the term *halal*, parallel to the Jewish concept of kosher (*kashrut*), is with respect to dietary regulations, and most specifically with reference to the humane slaughtering of animals. While the specifics of *halal* butchering are spelled out more fully in the hadith literature, its fundamental basis can be found in the following verse of the Qur'an.

> He has only forbidden you carrion, blood, pig's meat, and animals over which any name other than God's has been invoked. But if anyone is forced to eat such things out of hunger, rather than desire or excess, he commits no sin: God is most merciful and forgiving. (2:173)

The most familiar aspect of these regulations is with respect to the prohibition against eating pork, and, while the intention and meaning of this verse appear quite clear, readers are warned against taking an overly rigid approach to the interpretation of these regulations. Simply put, eating pork is preferable to starvation. This is just one example of a fundamental precept that is repeated in various ways throughout the Qur'an and that is an essential prerequisite for understanding shariah—that there is to be no hardship in religion (2:185).

The four foundations for the practice of shariah were articulated in the *Risalah* of al-Shafi'i (d. 820): as the Qur'an; the sunnah of the Prophet, as accessible through biographical works (*sira*) and the hadith collections; analogy (*qiyas*); and the consensus (*ijma*) of the community (Kamali 2003: 4-6). The first two of these foundations are documentary in nature, and as described in the previous section, also form the basis for *tafsir*. Kamali suggests that the justification for these two foundations can be found in the Qur'an (38).

> You who believe, obey God and the Messenger, and those in authority among you. If you are in dispute over any matter, refer it to God and the Messenger, if you truly believe in God and the Last Day: that is better and fairer in the end. (4:59)

The second two foundations are more strictly methodological, the first of which is based on the precepts of logical analysis, and the second of which relies on shared understanding.

With respect to the Qur'an as the primary source of shariah, it is critical to point out that it is not primarily a legal text. As Sardar reports, Said Ramadan identifies

> only 70 injunctions regarding family affairs, 70 on civil matters, 30 on penal law, 13 on jurisdiction and procedure, 10 on constitutional law, 25 on international relations, and 10 on economic and financial matters. (2003: 70)

This amounts to only about 10 percent of the Qur'an (Kamali 2003: 25).

In searching for guidance in the Qur'an, jurists are faced with the challenge that some verses are clear in meaning, while others are speculative or ambiguous. Similarly, there are verses that briefly cover general principles and those that spell matters out in great detail. Irrespective of the difficulties associated with interpreting the Qur'an, its primacy is associated with its revealed nature and its inimitability.

As with the Qur'an, the sunnah is considered to represent divine inspiration (Kamali 2003: 63). The critical issue for shariah is that there can be no conflict between the Qur'an and the sunnah; the sunnah can confirm or reiterate the Qur'an, offer an explanation or clarification, or express a ruling regarding a matter on which the Qur'an is silent. As described in the previous section, the substance of the sunnah, especially as collected in the hadith literature, is almost secondary to the matter of being able to establish the legitimate origin of the opinion being expressed.

The use of analogy (*qiyas*) is based on the recognition that new conditions might arise that bear some resemblance to previous conditions, but for which there is no clear solution provided by the Qur'an or sunnah. Four criteria are set out: the existence of an original case in which a ruling was provided, the existence of a new case requiring a ruling, the effective cause which is common to both cases, and the rule which can be applied to both. Kamali provides the example of the extension of the prohibition against drinking wine in the Qur'an (5:90) to the use of narcotic drugs (2003: 267-68). With respect to the first two criteria, the original case involved drinking wine and the new case involves taking drugs. The effective cause linking these two cases is intoxication and therefore the appropriate ruling is prohibition. The use of analogy is one of the key components of the application of personal reasoning to the process of interpretation.

The appeal to consensus (*ijma*) constitutes a sort of democratic check against the overuse or abuse of personal reasoning, because it places the basis for the authority of interpretation firmly in the social and political fabric of the Islamic community (Kamali 2003: 228). Those who participate in the establishment of consensus must be morally upright individuals, they must be qualified to express an informed opinion, and the opinion agreed upon must be free of pernicious innovation (234). Even though consensus is still viewed as essential element of shariah, precedence has generally been given to the agreements reached among the companions and successors of the Prophet. However, given that the opportunity for sharing ideas is increasingly being facilitated by the presence of ubiquitous global communication networks, it is reasonable to suggest that the process of consensus will likely emerge as the most vibrant and unpredictable aspect of shariah in the coming years.

Within the context of this elaborate multistep process of adapting to change, the practice of interpreting the Qur'an can be seen as a necessary but not a sufficient component in the search for guidance. One hazard that emerges from this realization, especially when coupled with the doctrinal position of the inimitability of the Qur'an, is that the interpretation of the Qur'an might receive less attention than it warrants, as judges and ordinary citizens place a greater emphasis on the sunnah and on the rulings of the canonical schools. Another potential hazard is that people might assume that everything we can learn from the Qur'an has already been documented by previous generations of commentators. Like some of the other scholars mentioned in the previous section, I am advocating for a renewed effort to return to the Qur'an as a source—one that is continuous and inexhaustible. There are two further matters to be mentioned in this discussion that were developed more fully within the context of shariah, but which play an essential role in interpreting the Qur'an: personal reasoning (*ijtihad*) and abrogation (*naskh*).

Kamali explains that personal reasoning is the mechanism through which the harmony between revelation and reason is established and maintained (2003: 468). The root of the word *ijtihad* is the same as that for jihad—both of which capture the idea of struggling, or applying great effort. Irrespective of the result obtained, the obligation resides in the attempt. Hallaq reports that the Prophet said: "If the judge exercised his *ijtihad* and reached the correct result, he is rewarded twice; if he is wrong then only once" (1997: 120). One of the great myths that has informed much popular opinion around the subject of personal reasoning, and one that has served to inhibit the development and practice of interpretation, is the idea that there was an official closing of the doors of *ijtihad* that accompanied, or was a consequence of, the establishment of the canonical law schools. As Abou El Fadl points out, the objective of this exercise was to stop the proliferation of schools, rather than halt the process of individual interpretation (2001: 66). Consistent with the understanding of shariah presented here, the practice of personal reasoning is essential to the continued wellbeing of the Islamic community.

While the word abrogation can mean cancellation, omission or even forgetting, its sense within exegesis and jurisprudence is more akin to the notion of substitution or replacement (Kamali 2003: 202-27). As John Burton explains, abrogation in the Qur'an has both an internal and an external sense (2001: 11). Externally, the Qur'an, and by extension Islam, is described as replacing the scripture and religious framework of Judaism and Christianity, which had been previously established for set periods (13:38) and were now being replaced by Islam as the last and final religion (33:40). From an internal perspective Saeed explains that there are four categories of abrogation, reflecting the act of replacing a verse or ruling in one source by a verse or ruling in the same or an alternate source, as follows: Qur'an by Qur'an, Qur'an by sunnah, sunnah by Qur'an and sunnah by sunnah. The relative legitimacy and precise mechanism of each of these possibilities are still hotly debated among Muslim scholars and jurists, but, for present purposes, understanding the idea that one verse or ruling in the Qur'an can be replaced by another is critical for developing a thorough appreciation of the contents of the fourth surah.

Among the direct references to the process of abrogation in the Qur'an, the following verse appears to clearly suggest that the act of replacement is consistent with the expression of divine will: "Any revelation We cause to be superseded or forgotten, We replace with something better or similar" (2:106). Some early commentators have suggested that there are as many as 500 cases of abrogation in the Qur'an, but eventually this number was drastically reduced, with al-Suyuti suggesting just twenty instances and Shah Walliullah (d. 1762) stating that there are only five legitimate cases (Saeed 2006: 78). As implied above, the act of replacement can occur with respect to either the wording of a particular verse or the ruling it represents. Thus there arise three possibilities: both the wording and the ruling can be abrogated, just the ruling, or just the wording. Burton refers to the first of these alternatives as the exegetical sense and the second as the juristic sense (2001: 17). While he does not label the third type, where the wording is replaced but the ruling is not, I will refer to this as the textual sense.

As an illustration of this third sense of abrogation, Burton uses the example of the so-called Stoning Verse. In the Qur'an, the recommendation with respect to punishing fornicators and adulterers is described in one instance merely by stating that the parties should be punished, without indicating exactly how this punishment should be carried out (4:15-16), while elsewhere the punishment is spelled out as striking them one hundred times (24:2). According to tradition, the companions of the Prophet insisted that there originally had been a verse prescribing the stoning to death of adulterers, with Umar, the second successor to Muhammad, urging Muslims not to forget this verse, suggesting that both he and his immediate predecessor Abu Bakr had put this ruling into practice (Burton 2001: 17). The fact that the Stoning Verse no longer appeared in the Qur'an was not viewed as an adequate justification to discontinue or ignore a practice apparently established in the Prophetic tradition. I refer to this type of abrogation as the textual sense, in order to capture the idea that while a ruling no longer appears in the book, it does appear to exist in the text. The concept I am trying to get across here is that the physical book is not capable of capturing the entire essence of the religion as it was originally revealed and established. Stated another way, the text of Islam is not the same as the book we know as the Qur'an.

As a final point before moving on to the next section, viewing the interpretation of the Qur'an as one step within the broader context of searching the documentary sources of Islam for guidance with respect to dealing with contemporary social conditions, shariah "does not restrict the liberty of the individual to investigate and express an opinion" (Kamali 2003: 31).

The Fourth Surah

The fourth surah of the Qur'an, referred to as *The Women* (*al-Nisa*), contains 176 verses and is generally thought to consist of material from the late Madinan period. It is listed in the standard Egyptian edition as the ninety-second surah to be revealed, and in the Nöldeke-Schwally ordering it is number one hundred. At about half the length of the second surah (*The Cow*), surah 4 is the second longest surah in the Qur'an, being about 10 per cent longer than surah 3 (*The Family of Imran*), which, even though it contains more verses (200), fills about fifteen pages in the Abdel Haleem translation, as compared to seventeen pages for surah 4.

With respect to its overall structure and thematic content, Mathias Zahniser summarizes the range of scholarly opinion on this matter by stating that at best the fourth surah has been viewed as a "stream-of-consciousness discourse," while at worst it has been seen as "disjointed and confused" (1997: 72-73). A major part of my motivation for studying and writing about the Qur'an stems from the fact that, in spite of centuries of scholarship by Muslims and non-Muslims, the meager handful of fulsome and holistic approaches to the study of the Qur'an are overshadowed by mainstream efforts that are informed either by the simplistic and reductionist view that the interpretation of the Qur'an should reflect its seemingly atomistic and fragmented structure, or by the equally misplaced and inappropriate expectation that the Qur'an should reflect chronological ordering or at least some level of narrative continuity (Reda 2010). The objective of this section is to provide a brief overview of the structure and content of the fourth surah, and to show that the surah illustrates much greater structural and thematic integrity than has generally been recognized.

In the introduction to his translation of this surah, Yusuf Ali observes that, thematically, *The Women* deals on one hand with the rights of individual families and on the other hand with the recalcitrance of the larger family, namely, the Muslim community in Madina (2004: 182). He goes on to suggest that the material related to these themes is distributed over eight sections, each with a particular emphasis:

4:1-14 – women and orphans
4:15-42 – rights and goodness
4:43-70 – false gods and the authority of the Prophet
4:71-91 – self-defence

4:92-104 – caution against killing
4:105-126 – treachery and the lure of evil
4:127-152 – women and orphans
4:153-176 – where the People of the Book went wrong

This division of the surah reflects the fact that, rather than trying to provide a detailed linguistic, structural or thematic analysis of the surah, Yusuf Ali is primarily interested in providing a concise subject guide for potential readers.

By contrast, Zahniser sets out to perform a systematic structural analysis of the surah, based on the assumption:

> (1) that the canonical text of the Qur'an, whatever its historical development may have been, has an integrity of its own and commensurate impact on its readers and hearers; and (2) that, since position is hermeneutic, attention to composition and structure can contribute significantly to understanding the meaning of the sura. (1997: 72)

Among other things, these assumptions suggest that we need to accept the Qur'an as it is, viewing its content and structure as purposive rather than accidental or arbitrary, and that we need to use the Qur'an as it has come down to us as the basis for understanding it. As he goes on to state: "What looks like disorganization to one culture might be clearly organized by the standards and conventions of another" (1997: 73, n. 7).

Zahniser takes his lead from the work of Pakistani scholar Amin Ahsan Islahi (d. 1997), who wrote in Urdu, and whose ideas have been made available to English readers through the writings of Mustansir Mir (1986). Using an inductive method, Islahi suggests that the fourth surah divides into three thematic units: social reform (4:1-43), the

Islamic community and its opponents (4:44-126) and conclusion (4:127-176), while identifying the overall theme
of the surah as "factors that make for cohesion in a Muslim
society" (Mir 1986: 47). While it is difficult to identify a
specific formulation of the inductive method, analyses of
this type have been used to great effect in the study of the
Bible as well as other literary works (Beekman et al. 1981).
Among other things, this method starts from the position
that the structure and content of a work are in some sense
purposive and then sets out to find clues to support that
notion. As has been discussed, much analysis of the Qur'an
has been predicated on the assumption that there is no
large-scale structural coherence to the text and therefore
the proper unit of analysis is the individual verse.

Compared to Islahi, Zahniser divides the surah into five
rather than three sections, with the first and fifth sections
matching Islahi's first and third sections, with respect to the
range of verses to be included in each section. Zahniser divides Islahi's middle section into three parts, identifying a
central section on the theme of armed conflict that Islahi
appears to have either missed or chosen not to highlight.
Also, Zahniser uses the subject of the various sections (e.g.,
women) as the means of identification, rather than using the
intention of dealing with the subject (e.g., social reform).

I – Women Block (1-43)
II – intermediary material (44-70)
III – Battle Block (71-104)
IV – intermediary material (105-126)
V – Women Cluster (127-135) – hollow portion (136-
175) – Women Verse (176)

At a purely arithmetical level, Zahniser points out that, sections II and IV are about the same length, and that sections I and V are the same length, about two and one-half times longer than the intermediary sections (1997: 80). The central section is about double the length of the intermediary sections. Whether the amount of text devoted to each subject can be interpreted as an indicator of the relative importance of each subject is an open question, but at the very least the obvious structural symmetry not only helps the reader keep track of what is being discussed, it also suggests that there is an integral relationship between the various subjects.

The establishment of this overall thematic division of the surah is based on clues provided in the more microstructural elements of the text, such as rhyme scheme, formulas of address and recurrent phrases. The use of rhyme scheme as an indicator of structure, while relying on familiarity with the Arabic text, does not require a comprehensive understanding of the Arabic language. The sound patterns would be easily recognizable to anyone who undertook a careful listening to the recitation of the surah. As exemplified in studies by Angelika Neuwirth (1981) and Neal Robinson (2003a), Zahniser's analysis of the rhyme scheme suggests, for example, that a link can be established between the Women Block and the Women Verse because they display the same rhythmic pattern. He also points out that verse 3 displays a rhyme pattern which is different from those occurring in the rest of the surah, adding that he has been unable to determine the significance of this difference (1997: 75, n. 20).

At the simplest level, we might conclude that this unique occurrence has no particular significance. Alternately, it could be being used as an attention getting device—a way to cause the reader/listener to pause at this point. Going further, we might suggest that this verse was revealed separately from the verses surrounding it, and that it was later inserted here as a means of providing greater detail on the adjacent subject matter, thus constituting an interpolation. The interpretation of this verse (4:3) is covered in greater detail in the next chapter.

Regarding formulas of address, Zahniser observes that among the five formulas that are used in the fourth surah, all but one of these play a role in structuring the overall narrative (1997: 78). For example, the formula "You who believe" occurs nine times, at fairly regular intervals (verses 19, 29, 43, 59, 71, 94, 135, 136 and 144). In contrast, special significance can be attached to the use of the vocative "People" (Abdel Haleem), or as it is often expressed, "Oh You People" (Zahniser) or "Oh mankind" (Yusuf Ali; Pickthall), which occurs only three times, once at the very beginning of the surah (verse 1), and then again twice (verses 170 and 174) at the end of the surah. As this formula is the first thing that people hear following the *basmalah*, it is logical to conclude that when the formula appears again, the reader might anticipate that its occurrence is signalling the end of the surah. However, what in fact takes place is that a short sequence of verses (171-173) is inserted here before the formula is repeated, to then bring the surah to a close. The use of this deceptive or false ending has the effect of shifting the listener's attention and highlighting the content of the short inserted sequence. The interpretation of these verses is discussed in the chapter on hypocrites.

Parallel to the use of repeated formulas of address is the use recurrent phrases, both as a means of structuring the overall narrative and as a way to establish linkage between specific passages and sections. For example, the phrase "They ask you [Prophet] for a ruling," which occurs in verses 127 and 176 links the Women Cluster to the Women Verse and suggests that the material between these two verses may constitute a thematic unit. Even more striking is the use of these nearly identical verses.

> God does not forgive the joining of partners with Him: anything less than that He forgives to whoever He will, but anyone who joins partners with God has concocted a tremendous sin. (4:48)

> God does not forgive the worship of others beside Him— though He does forgive whoever He will for lesser sins— for whoever does this has gone far, far astray (4:116)

The first instance (verse 48) occurs in section II and the second instance occurs in section IV, thereby suggesting that these intermediary sections (Zahniser does not provide a specific subject label for these sections) are thematically parallel. Closer examination reveals that section II deals more specifically with the People of the Book, while section IV addresses those from a traditional Arabian religious background. In both cases, it is the error of polytheism that is highlighted, and both of these sections, together with further elaboration contained in the hollow portion of section V, can be viewed as a more general discussion of the very specific and detailed warning provided in the specially de-marcated sequence (verses 171-173) at the end of the surah.

As a final example of the use of repeated phrases, the phrase "Everything in the heavens and earth belongs to God" is repeated six times (verses 126, 131 [2x], 132, 170 and 171). All but one of these occurrences (verse 126) can be found in section V, with Zahniser identifying the single use outside the section as a case of concatenation.

The term concatenation, also known as chaining (Abdul-Raof 2003), refers to the literary effect of using the same word, or words, in two distinct clauses, in separate places within a text, to form a linkage between them (Trask 2000). This device is often used as a substitute for the longer transi-tional text segments (e.g., paragraphs at the end of chapters) that we are accustomed to seeing in more narrative forms of writing. Unlike the use of foreshadowing, which might employ the use of metaphor, concatenation is a more literal and direct means of providing seemingly innocuous but at the same time very clear hints to the reader that what they are now reading is somehow linked to something they have read earlier in the text. Like foreshadowing, it raises an expecta-tion in the reader, as admirably expressed in Anton Chekhov's advice to an aspiring writer, that: "If in the first chapter you say that a gun hung on the wall, in the second, or third chapter it must without fail be discharged" (qtd. in Abbott 2008: 60).

Consequently, consistent with the premise of the induc-tive approach, no element of a text should be viewed as su-perfluous or independent. Even though the linkages might not be apparent, even to several generations of readers, the failure to identify structural or thematic links should be identified in the first place with our lack of understanding and not with some inherent flaw in the text.

GIVEN the emphasis on these micro-structural elements, it might seem reasonable to assume that the real building blocks of the Qur'an are not the verses or the surahs, but rather the individual phrases, or what are referred to technically as cola (s. colon). This makes a great deal of sense when you think in terms of the oral Qur'an, with cola (word sequences) corresponding to units of speech—the way we hear the text. At the same time it is important to realize that these units are put together in complex ways to establish the overall thematic structure of the Qur'an. To repeat Zahniser's observation: position is hermeneutic. The following example will provide some insight into the way that structural complexity is achieved.

In a footnote, Zahniser identifies the sequence of verses from 137 to 143 as demonstrating a chiastic structure (1997: 75, n. 15). As I have demonstrated elsewhere (Campbell 2009), chiasmus is used regularly throughout the Qur'an as a framework for thematic structuring, and given the fact that the primary means of transmission for the Qur'an was, and to a large extent still is oral, chiasmus provides an effective mnemonic device to aid recitation, just as is the case with the Torah and Homer's *Iliad* and *Odyssey*. Zahniser provides no further detail, but here is my suggestion for one possible way to demarcate and interpret this sequence.

A – waivering in faith (137)
  B – God punishes (138)
    C – seeking power (139)
      D – Hell for hypocrites and disbelievers (140)
    C' – seeking power (141)
  B' – God deceives (142)
A' – waivering in faith (143)

This is an odd-numbered chiasm (seven elements) pointing towards a central message (D), with the components of the structure aligning directly with the numbered verses, which is not always the case. The presence of a chiasm does not necessarily imply precise mathematical parallelism with respect to the number of words, phrases or verses. While these textual elements can provide valuable clues, the primary characteristic for identifying a chiasm is the presence of reverse parallelism with respect to themes. In this instance, the bracketing verses (A-A') both deal with those who waiver in faith, with the final verse (A') using the word waiver directly and the initial verse (A) referring to those who continually change their minds. The next pair of verses (B-B') deals with the exercise of God's power, in the first instance (B) to punish the hypocrites, and in the second instance (B') to deceive those who believe they can deceive God. The pair of verses (C-C') that directly bracket the central message addresses the idea of allying yourself with one group or another as a means of seeking advantage. As a demonstration of the fact that thematic pairings within a chiasm can vary quite significantly in length, verse 141 (C'), with seventy-three words, is three times longer than verse 139 (C), with twenty-four words. Finally, the central verse (D) combines the various elements that have been introduced in the bracketing verses, warning the faithful not to fall in with the hypocrites and disbelievers, lest they become like them, and then with them will be condemned to hell.

One conclusion we can draw from this analysis is that there is an unquestionable structural integrity to the surah, and that, whether the surah was revealed all at once or pieced together from a number of separate revelations, it should be treated in a holistic manner. Following Zahniser's analysis, we might speculate that the inherent logic of the surah appears to be that because there are those who would associate others with God, battle in defense of Islam might be necessary, and as a consequence of the loss of (male) life, or even long absence, associated with combat, special care needs to be taken in providing for women. Through the discussions of women, war and hypocrites contained in the following chapters, I try to provide ample evidence to allow readers to determine if there is any merit in this hypothesis.

Women

Introduction

Juliane Hammer remarks:

> Quite possibly, a rethinking of the roles of women and men as derived from the Qur'an can be described as a litmus test for Muslims' ability to be modern and adapt their religious interpretation and practice to the "standards" of Western modernity. (2008: 448)

While this statement might appear to represent a rather controversial starting point for the discussions that follow, I am not interested in establishing whether the adaptation being suggested by Hammer is a laudable or even remotely desirable goal. What I am interested in is the implicit message in her statement that what is presented in the Qur'an is more comparable to modern Western views on gender roles than it is to those reflected in the social practices and interpretive frameworks of contemporary Islamic communities. Irrespective of whatever else one might read into Hammer's remark, I include it here in order to again emphasize the need for people to look to the Qur'an as the primary source of their understanding of Islam.

As outlined in the previous chapter, Zahniser identifies three sections in the fourth surah that deal with women: the Women Block (4:1-43), the Women Cluster (4:127-135) and the Women Verse (4:176). With respect to the content of these sections, the longer opening sequence contains discussions of property, orphans, marriage, inheritance, licit and illicit sexual relations, and the establishment and maintenance of good relationships between men and women, among family members and between people and God. The middle cluster presents a summary of these same issues and the final section (a single verse) deals only with inheritance. Reflecting the principle themes that emerge in these verses, in what follows, major sections are devoted to the topics of marriage, lewdness, wife beating and hijab, while the remainder of this introduction deals with the Qur'anic presentation of women more broadly and the subject of inheritance.

Even though only one woman is actually named in the Qur'an (Mary, the mother of Jesus), several others, whose stories would be familiar from the Torah, are referred to in conjunction with their husbands or other prominent male figures that are named. While the presentation of these women in the Qur'an is similar to the way that they are portrayed in Hebrew scripture, some important differences do occur. For example, in contrast to the account provided in Genesis, in the Qur'an (2:30-37, 20:115-123, 7:11-25), not only are Adam and his wife created together, but they are also tempted together by Satan in the Garden. These two points merit further comment. First, the Qur'an does not replicate the ontological hierarchy between the sexes that has informed historical views on gender roles in the West. Second, women are not viewed as the source of sin or as morally weaker beings. If anything, Adam is portrayed as carrying the greater share of the burden; in one verse (20:120) he alone is tempted.

In what might be viewed as a counterexample to the portrayal of Eve, the efforts of the wife of the Egyptian vizier (known as Zulaykha) to seduce Joseph are recounted in great detail in the twelfth surah—the longest continuous narrative in the Qur'an (Campbell 2009: 59-76). The idea of woman-as-seductress is emphasized in this story, with the treachery of women being mentioned seven times in a short sequence of verses (e.g., 12:28). At the same time, even though he is found to be blameless, Joseph chooses to be imprisoned as way of avoiding evil, admitting that he had to struggle to resist Zulaykha's advances (12:33-35). Roded points out that through the interpretive history of this story Zulaykha is transformed from dangerous sexual predator to ideal spouse (2006: 531-32). In these accounts, she is punished for her attempt to subvert Joseph's innocence, redeemed and then rewarded for her unreserved love for Joseph, becoming his wife and the mother of his children.

Perhaps the strongest female character portrayed in the Qur'an is the pagan Queen of Sheba (known as Bilqis). The story of her interaction with Solomon, known for his wisdom and judgment (27:22-44), stands out for several reasons, foremost of which might be that it contains a unique occurrence of the *basmalah* (Campbell 2009: 88-90). Furthermore, the sequence of events demonstrates the value of consultation, the wisdom of diplomacy over war and the omnipotence and omniscience of God, to whom Bilqis ultimately submits. Roded remarks that, in spite of her demonstrated wisdom and leadership, Muslim commentators do not seem to have considered the possibility of holding Bilqis up as an example for the roles of women in their societies (2006: 533).

With respect to women who would be contemporaries of the Prophet, and who would likely be known to his initial audience, the story of the wife of Abu Lahab stands out in that it is one of the most brutal and graphic passages in the Qur'an.

> May the hands of Abu Lahab be ruined! May he be ruined too! Neither his wealth nor his gains will help him: he will burn in the Flaming Fire—and so will his wife, the firewood carrier, with a palm-fibre rope around her neck. (111:1-4)

This short surah contains the only example of outright condemnation of specific individuals in the Qur'an, and it should leave no doubt that men and women are viewed as equally capable of committing evil and equally deserving of punishment.

LOOKING PAST references to specific individuals, in the first verse of the fourth surah, and in several other places (e.g., 7:189, 35:11, 49:13, 51:49, 53:45, 76:39, 78:8 and 92:3), men and women are said to have been created together from one soul, destined to live together, to procreate and to be mindful of God. The moral and religious equality of men and women is described most thoroughly in the following verse.

> For men and women who are devoted to God—believing men and women, obedient men and women, truthful men and women, steadfast men and women, humble men and women, charitable men and women, fasting men and women, chaste men and women, men and women who remember God often—God has prepared forgiveness and a rich reward. (33:35)

While this verse would appear to suggest that men and women are equally and independently accountable before God, other verses (36:55-56, 43:70) suggest that a woman's fate in the afterlife is tied to that of her husband (Roded 2006: 524). Still other verses are troubling because they appear to promise believers that in Paradise they will be paired with "beautiful-eyed maidens" (52:20), "maidens restraining their glances, untouched beforehand by man" (55:56), and "nubile, well-matched companions" (78:33). As will become clear in the section on terrorism in the final chapter of this book, the interpretation of these particular verses has become a key component in motivating male suicide-bombers.

Despite of the apparent emphasis on gender equity, Roded is of the opinion that symbolically in the Qur'an women are depicted as weak, flawed or passive (2006: 524). She bases this view on the fact that women are often portrayed along with orphans and the infirm as being helpless (4:75, 98), and on the fact that menstruation is viewed as a mark of illness and impurity (2:222, 4:43). Further, women are associated with the earth and with man's mastery over nature, as evidenced in the oft-cited verse: "Your wives are your fields, so go into your fields whichever way you like" (2:223). At the same time, however, the Qur'an judges the preference for the birth of sons over daughters as being among the sins of the pagans (16:58-59), and it identifies the practice of burying newborn girls alive as an evil, unnatural act (81:8-9).

Roded observes that 80 per cent of the legal material in the Qur'an refers to women (2006: 527). As will become clear throughout this chapter, the bulk of this material deals with marriage, divorce and inheritance—the rights of women with respect to their husbands and families. Surely it is reasonable to suggest that whatever the present state and perception of women's place within Islam might be, for its part, the text of the Qur'an reflects a concerted effort to improve the status and treatment of women.

DAVID POWERS indicates that inheritance is dealt with in two sets of verses, the first of which he refers to as the Bequest Verses (2:180-182, 2:240, 5:106-107), and the second (4:7, 4:11-12, 4:176), which were revealed following the Battle of Uhud, dealing with rules for the division of property (2002: 518-19). While the Bequest Verses allowed leeway with respect to how and to whom property would be allocated through a valid (appropriately witnessed) last will and testament, the verses contained in the fourth surah constrained this process in three ways. First, they stipulated that both men and women are to receive their share (4:7). Second, they laid out the specifics as to how property was to be divided, based on familial relationship and gender (4:11-12). Third, they provided a mechanism to deal with cases that fell outside normal circumstances, such as when an individual dies leaving no parents or children (4:176). While the precise application of these principles has led to the development of an elaborate set of precedents and procedures, one overriding principle is that, other things being equal, men are to inherit double the share of women. We might question how such a distribution reflects the equal treatment of men and women. There does not appear to be much disagreement among commentators on this issue, with the predominant opinion taking the form expressed by Ingrid Mattson, that: "The greater inheritance share of males, therefore, although not equal, is considered equitable because of their greater financial responsibility within the nuclear and extended family" (2008: 216).

A second issue related to inheritance is raised in the initial section of surah, where we read that: "it is not lawful for you to inherit women against their will" (4:19). The message contained in this brief statement is quite clear: women are not to be treated as chattel or booty.

The importance of understanding what the Qur'an has to say about inheritance is related to the importance of understanding the context in which the text was revealed and to an appreciation of the fact that in the transition from a pre-Islamic to an Islamic value system, the political, religious and social orders were integrated as they had never been before.

Marriage

Abdel Haleem states that: "Islam is the religion of marriage and only allows divorce in order to create better marriages" (1999: 42). Marriage is a divine institution designed to allow men and women to live a tranquil life together full of mutual love and kindness (30:21), as opposed to remaining single (24:32), and especially in contrast to the Christian ideal of celibacy and monasticism, which the Qur'an denounces as a human invention (57:27). Following a general discussion of marriage and divorce, this section deals with three controversial topics: polygamy, the wives of the Prophet and temporary marriage.

From a moral perspective, marriage is viewed as the legitimate institution within which men and women can satisfy their sexual desires, with the Qur'an advocating marital fidelity and speaking out strongly against sexual indiscretion (Motzki 2003: 277). Marriage is the mechanism through which kinship bonds are established and maintained (25:54), and it is the appropriate means for bringing children into the world and providing a proper environment for their upbringing (7:189, 16:72). Importantly, in a society where men often lost their lives while trading or making war, marriage provided the community with a way to take care of widowed and orphaned females (4:3).

Men are prohibited from marrying women that are closely related to them (4:22-24), and they may not marry idolatresses (2:221) or disbelievers (60:10). The actual process of getting married is uncomplicated, consisting of a proposal (2:235), which the man makes to the woman's guardian, the preparation of a contract by the guardian

(2:237), the payment of the bride-gift (2:236), which becomes the bride's property, and the consummation of the marriage, which seals the contract (Motzki 2003: 278). The Qur'an describes husbands and wives as each other's garments (2:187), and only forbids intercourse during a woman's menstrual period, times of obligatory fasting and during the pilgrimage.

In addition to their wives, men were allowed to have sexual intercourse with their female slaves, as suggested in several verses in the Qur'an (e.g., 16:71, 70:30), where such women are referred to euphemistically as "what your right hand possesses" (Brockopp 2001: 396). Interestingly, while the secondary literature often refers to a man's sexual partners outside of marriage as concubines, the Arabic word for concubine does not appear in the Qur'an. The status of children born to concubines is not discussed in the Qur'an, but later Islamic jurists would declare them to be legitimate.

THE REGULATIONS pertaining to divorce are discussed quite extensively in two long passages (2:229-240, 65:1-7). A man can simply pronounce that he wants a divorce, but it does not become final until his wife has completed three menstrual periods, followed by an additional waiting period of three months in order to ensure that she is not pregnant. During this time, a man may withdraw his initial declaration and at a later period again seek a divorce. If he changes his mind again, after the third time, he may no longer retract his declaration, and if he wants to remarry his wife, he must wait until she has married another man and then divorced him. Reconciliation is always the goal (4:35). A woman cannot obtain a divorce through pronouncement. As Motzki explains, if she could, it would give her an inappropriate level of control over a component of his property (2003: 280). The man has invested in the marriage through the provision of the bride-gift and if he wants to give that up, then that is his prerogative.

In order for a woman to instigate a divorce, she must seek it through mutual consent whereby the husband agrees to let her go in return for the value of the bride-gift and any other gifts he has given her. Clearly, this sort of divorce is not in the best economic interests of the woman. If a man divorces his wife while she is still breastfeeding his child, then he is responsible to maintain the woman and the child, until the child is two years old, and must pay his ex-wife a wage for breastfeeding. There is no stigma attached to divorce in Islam, with both parties being encouraged to remarry and carry on their legitimate sex life (Abdel Haleem 1999: 57).

THE FIRST controversy to be discussed pertains to the number of women that a man is allowed to marry.

> If you fear that you will not deal fairly with orphan girls, you may marry whichever [other] women seem good to you, two, three, or four. If you fear that you cannot be equitable [to them], then marry only one, or your slave(s): that is more likely to make you avoid bias. (4:3)

Perhaps the first observation to be made about this verse is that it does not provide a straightforward unencumbered instruction or declaration with respect to marrying more than one woman. Rather, it embeds the permission within a complex rhetorical structure that stands out even with respect to the fact that, as mentioned in the final section of the previous chapter, it employs a unique rhyme scheme within the surah. More obvious to readers of the Qur'an in translation, the parallel use of the phrase "if you fear" in this verse links it to the Beating Verse (4:34), discussed later in this chapter, which is the only other verse in the Qur'an to employ this coupling. While it is difficult to determine what if any significance should be attributed to the use of this linguistic construction, the fact that both of these verses deal with controversial matters regarding women would appear to suggest that the text is illustrating a level of self-awareness about the sensitivity and importance of gender issues in establishing a new Islamic social order.

Looking more directly at the structure, this verse contains parallel if-then statements and a conclusion. Both of the conditionals and the conclusion deal with equity, and both of the consequences deal with marriage. The first statement suggests that if a man fears he will be inequitable to orphan girls, should he marry one or more of them, then he should marry one, or up to four, otherwise available eligible women. If in contemplating this option, a man fears he will be inequitable to multiple wives, the second statement suggests he should marry only one, or his slaves. The final statement reinforces the wisdom of this second option by suggesting that in choosing this option it will make it easier for the man to avoid treating his wives inequitably. Leaving aside the matter of slaves, which as we saw above carries with it another series of problems, one of the keys to understanding this verse is the fact that it presupposes the existence of available orphan girls.

The preceding verse (4:2) warns against taking the property of orphans, substituting goods of lesser value for theirs and consuming their goods along with your own. The content of this verse would seem to suggest that a child had just become orphaned, or that an orphan had reached the age of independence, and that a particular person was in a position to determine how the orphan, and any property the orphan was entitled to, should be dealt with. In a note attached to verse 4:3, Abdel Haleem observes that in pre-Islamic times, men would often marry orphan girls as a means of taking their property (2005: 50). Thus, both the context and the co-text provide the necessary background within which to understand the conditional framework of the verse and the fact that the initial subjects are orphan girls. In the subsequent verse (4:4), men are instructed to give women their dowry upon marriage and, while this verse does not specify what kind of women are being referred to, following on from the preceding verses, the message would appear to be that a man should not look to a woman, especially one whose social status might be questionable (viz., an orphan), to bring him property through marriage. Rather that the onus is on him to provide a gift to a prospective wife, so that she may acquire property of her own.

Returning to the first statement in the verse, and viewing it within the context of inheritance and distribution of wealth, a more conservative understanding of the permission to marry up to four women would appear to entail the condition that a man could not only afford to marry this number of women, but that he could ensure the equitable distribution of that wealth among his wives. Later in the surah (4:129), we read that despite a man's best efforts he will never be able to treat all of his wives fairly, and even though this latter verse appears to be referring more to emotional and sexual attention, the overarching assessment of the human condition remains. While men are given the freedom to some extent to act in a way that matches their desires (acquisition of wealth through marriage rather than access to multiple sex partners), divine counsel suggests that through experience they will come to a different realization.

THE SECOND controversial topic concerns the number of the Prophet's wives (Stowasser 2006).

> [Prophet] We have made lawful for you the wives whose bride gift you have paid, and any slaves God has assigned to you through war, and the daughters of your uncles and aunts on your father's and mother's sides, who migrated with you. Also any believing woman who has offered herself to the Prophet and whom the Prophet wishes to wed—this is only for you [Prophet] and not the rest of the believers: We know exactly what We have made obligatory for them concerning their wives and slave-girls—so you should not be blamed: God is most forgiving, most merciful. (33:50)

This verse articulates a special set of rules for the Prophet with respect to the number and category of women available to him for marriage, thus setting him apart from other Muslims. However, as the following verse suggests, the Prophet's alternate social arrangements gave rise to certain difficulties.

> You may make any of [your women] wait and receive any of them as you wish, but you will not be at fault if you invite one whose turn you have previously set aside: this way it is more likely that they will be satisfied and will not be distressed and will all be content with what you have given them. God knows what is in your hearts: God is all knowing, forbearing. (33:51)

Not only does this verse suggest that the existence of multiple wives might give rise to jealousies and discontents, it also re-assures the Prophet that his efforts to deal with the logistics of his marital arrangements do not go unnoticed by God. The following verse appears to provide a more permanent solution to any problems that may arise.

> You [Prophet] are not allowed to take any further wives, nor to exchange the wives you have for others, even if these attract you with their beauty. But this does not apply to your slave-girls: God is watchful over all. (33:52)

Commentators have suggested that this final verse (33:52) must be interpreted as abrogating the earlier one (33:50), otherwise the text would appear to contain a contradiction (Stowasser 2006: 513-14). Another way of explaining this structure is to suggest that both verses were included as a way of explaining to readers how the actions permitted to the Prophet changed over the period of the revelation. At the very least, the fact that these three verses directly follow each other in the Qur'an would seem to provide evidence that the order in which various components of the text appear in the codified version does not necessarily reflect the order in which they were revealed/produced.

Based on the biographical source material it appears that Muhammad had a total of thirteen female partners, but several other women are mentioned in a variety of sources as being his concubines or female associates. Here is a list of Muhammad's widely acknowledged wives and concubines in the order in which they are reported to have become associated with him (their age at that time is given in brackets).

Khadija bint Khuwaylid (40)
Sawda bint Zama (30)
Aisha bint Abi Bakr (9)
Hafsa bint Umar (18)
Umm Salama bint al-Mughira (29)
Zaynab bint al-Khuzayma (30)
Juwayriyya (20)
Zaynab bint Jahsh (38)
Mariya the Copt (unknown)
Rayhana bint Zayd (unknown)
Umm Habiba bint Abi Sufyan (35)
Safiyya bint Huyayy (17)
Maymuna bint al-Harith (27)

With the exception of Aisha, all of the other women whom the Prophet married were either widowed or divorced.

Muhammad's first wife Khadija was a wealthy merchant who was twenty-five years his senior, and who had been twice widowed. Muhammad worked for Khadija, probably managing caravans, and most accounts suggest that she proposed to him. Their male children died in infancy and they had four daughters: Zaynab, Ruqayya, Umm Kulthum and Fatima. According to tradition Khadija is said to have sought the advice of her Christian cousin Waraqah ibn Nawful, when Muhammad was fearful and uncertain of how to proceed after receiving the first revelation (Ramadan 2007: 30). It was Waraqah who recognized that Muhammad was being called to prophethood.

Only after the death of Khadija in 619, following twenty-five years together, did Muhammad take more than one woman in marriage.

Sawda was the widow of Sakran ibn Amr, an early convert to Islam who had emigrated with his wife and a small group of Muslims to Abyssinia in order to avoid persecution, but who had died upon his return to Makkah. Sawda married the Prophet in 620 and emigrated with him to Madina.

Aisha was the daughter of Abu Bakr, a close associate of the Prophet and the individual who would become his immediate successor as political and religious leader of the Muslim community. Aisha married Muhammad in 623, when she was nine years old, and remained childless. As Denise Spellberg explains, Aisha's persona would focus early debates about Islamic identity and gender roles, especially through the controversies surrounding the story of her vindication from an accusation of adultery, her participation in the first civil war and efforts to characterize her as an exemplary female, comparable to Mary the mother of Jesus (2001: 56).

The story of the accusation of adultery appears for the first time almost two hundred years after the events it pertains to, as a means of providing a context for the revelation of a particular passage in the Qur'an (24:11-20). This passage does not mention Aisha by name, nor does it recount the accusation of adultery against her. Rather, the verses refer to the incident as "the lie," and the primary message emerging from the passage is the severity of the punishment that awaits those who slander an individual without producing four witnesses. Sunni commentators argued that the passage was revealed to vindicate Aisha, who had been wrongly accused, while Shia commentators argued that, while the passage did in fact refer to an accusation of adultery, the person accused was not Aisha, but rather Mariya the Copt. This conflict in interpretation reflects one element of the emerging sectarian division between Sunni and Shia, with the latter group viewing the Sunni interpretation as both an attempt to support Aisha's father Abu Bakr and a clear admission of Aisha's guilt. From a Shia perspective, Aisha was the enemy of Ali, who they regarded as the rightful successor to Muhammad (Afsaruddin 2008).

The second controversy pertains to Aisha's participation in the civil war between her allies and Ali, who was fighting to defend his position as fourth caliph and rightful successor to Muhammad. Her appearance at the so-called Battle of the Camel drew censure from both Sunni and Shia commentators, who argued that she should have stayed at home, which, in accordance with the Qur'an (33:33), would be the proper behaviour for the wife of the Prophet. This point of agreement between the sects greatly influenced later perceptions of the role of Muslim women as being focused in the home and avoiding involvement in political and military matters.

The third matter relates to Aisha's status as an exemplar of Islamic female ideals. The Qur'an makes it quite clear that Mary had been chosen by God above all women (3:42), and elsewhere it identifies Mary and the wife of Pharaoh (known as Asiya) as exemplary believing women, in contrast to the wives of Noah and Lot, who will both be condemned to the fire (66:9-12). Despite of her position as the wife of the Prophet, and her historical importance as a key source of information on the Prophet's life, Aisha's position, when compared with these other women, is rather ambivalent. As a result of the story of the lie and the disobedience associated with her participation in the Battle of the Camel, she never attains the status of Mary or Asiya, and even Khadija and Fatima emerge as more exemplary models of the ideal (religious) woman (Spellberg 2001: 59).

The issue of Aisha's age, both with respect to the fact that Muhammad was forty-three years her senior and that she was a child bride, does not figure very prominently in Islamic discourse, nor has it generated much wider scholarly attention. Her uniqueness as the only virgin to marry the Prophet has led some commentators to suggest that this attribute is a sign that she was selected specifically for the Prophet, and that in virtue of this fact she deserves the appellation of mother of the believers (Spellberg 2001). The controversies surrounding Aisha have attracted some recent attention, primarily as a result of the debate over whether the publication of a fictional account of the relationship between Muhammad and Aisha by Sherry Jones, called *The Jewel of Medina* (2008), would generate backlash from the Muslim community in the United States. In an afterword to her novel, the author recounts how publishing giant Random House entered a contract with her for two books and then, at least partially on the advice of a University of Texas academic who suggested that publishing the book might incite violence, backed out of the deal. The book was subsequently published by a small press in England, resulting in a firebombing of the publisher's home. Not long afterwards it was published in the United States and, apart from generating some less than kind reviews, it has not caused much of a stir.

Hafsa was the daughter of Umar ibn al-Khattab, who would serve as caliph from 634 to 644, and the widow of Khunays ibn Hudhafa. She married Muhammad in 625, but tradition suggests that he divorced her and then remarried her, based on the incident reported in the following verses (Rubin 2002: 398).

> The Prophet told something in confidence to one of
> his wives. When she disclosed it [to another wife] and
> God made this known to him, he confirmed part of it,
> keeping the rest to himself. When he confronted her
> with what she had done, she asked, "Who told you about
> this?" and he replied, "The All Knowing, the All Aware
> told me." If both of you [wives] repent to God—for your

hearts have deviated—[all will be well]; if you collabo-
rate against him, [be warned that] God will aid him, as
will Gabriel and all righteous believers, and the angels
too will back him. His Lord may well replace you with
better wives if the Prophet decides to divorce any of you:
wives who are devoted to God, true believers, devout,
who turn to Him in repentance and worship Him, given
to fasting, whether previously married or virgin. (66:3-5)

Hafsa is said to have possessed a private copy of the
Qur'an, based on a version that she heard directly from
the Prophet, which was used in preparation of the Uth-
manic codex (Leehmuis 2001). Apparently, this copy was
later destroyed by Marwan, the governor of Madina, in an
effort to avoid any conflicts over which version was to be
considered authoritative.

Umm Salama, who had several small children at the
time she married Muhammad in 626, was the widow of
Abu Salama, who had died of a wound inflicted at the Battle of Uhud. Zaynab bint al-Khuzayma had been divorced
by her first husband, and then lost her second husband (her
first husband's brother) in the Battle of Badr. She married
the Prophet in 626. Juwayriyya, the daughter of a tribal
chief, was captured during a raid in 627 and married Muhammad after her conversion to Islam. Zaynab bint Jahsh,
who was Muhammad's first cousin on his mother's side,
had been divorced by her first husband Zayd ibn Haritha
and married the Prophet in 627.

Mariya was a Coptic Christian, who had been sent to
Muhammad as a gift by the ruler of Egypt around 627.
Rayhana was captured during a raid on a Jewish tribe in

627, and remained a concubine until her death a few years later. Umm Habiba, the widow of an early convert to Islam, married the Prophet in 628. Safiyya, who was captured at Khaybar in 628, married Muhammad after she converted from Judaism. Upon his conversion to Islam, Muhammad's uncle Abbas offered him his sister-in-law Maymuna, who had recently been widowed. They were married in 629, when they returned to Madina following the performance of the minor pilgrimage (Ramadan 2007: 170).

The Qur'an appears to attribute a special status to the wives of the Prophet, when it states that: "The wives of Muhammad are the mothers of the believers" (33:6), and that for someone to marry a wife of the Prophet after he is gone, "would be grievous in God's eyes" (33:53). This differentiation takes on even more significance when it comes to the discussion of hijab in the final section of this chapter, giving rise to the question of whether the regulations apply to all women, or just to the wives of the Prophet.

FINALLY, the third controversy focuses on the matter of temporary marriage, which is a contractual arrangement through which a man can enter into a sexual relationship with an unmarried woman for a specified period, for a fee (Williams 2009: 232). Although not explicitly mentioned in the Qur'an, the basis for this practice is said to reside in a reference to a pre-Islamic practice in verse 4:24.

> If you wish to enjoy women through marriage, give
> them their bride-gift—this is obligatory—though if you

should choose mutually, after fulfilling this obligation, to do otherwise [with the bride-gift], you will not be blamed. (Abdel Haleem)

It is difficult to determine from this translation what pre-Islamic practice is being referred to. Rather, the verse appears to be suggesting that, after a husband has provided his wife with the bride-gift, it is up to them what they do with it once they are married. The following translation suggests an alternate understanding.

And those of whom you seek content (by marrying them), give them their portions (dowry) as a duty. And there is no sin for you in what you do by mutual agreement after the duty (has been done). (Pickthall)

This translation is open to a more liberal interpretation, suggesting that once a man has given a woman a bride-gift, in an effort to seek content (sexual satisfaction) from her, the two of them can go forward in whatever way they choose. Although not stated, apparently this could be taken to mean that, as a consequence of the bride-gift, the two are free to have legitimate sexual relations together, and that if they choose to terminate the relationship at some point, then they will not be judged to have sinned.

Historically the Sunni majority has viewed this practice as illegal, claiming that it had been outlawed by the caliph Umar. The Shia continue to contest this claim, not only on the basis of the reference in 4:24, but also on the fact that there is no prophetic hadith against the practice. They argue that while the purpose of permanent marriage is procreation, the purpose of temporary marriage is specifically sexual enjoyment. The practice has become more common in Iran since the revolution in 1979. Under such an arrangement, no maintenance or inheritance is due to the woman even if she becomes pregnant. Men, whether single or married, may enter as many of these arrangements as they choose, renewing them as often as the partners desire, but a women is only permitted to enter one marriage at a time, whether permanent or temporary. As Williams suggests, while this practice demonstrates a sort of convergence of morality, sexuality, religious rules, secular laws and cultural practices, it also highlights the tension between religion and popular culture in contemporary society (2006: 234).

Abou El Fadl reports on a similar arrangement recognized by religious authorities in Saudi Arabia (2001: 179). If a man enters into marriage with a woman with the intention of divorcing her after a certain amount of time, for example, while he is abroad on a student visa, and he does not disclose his intentions to her, then the marriage is considered to be legal. By contrast, if a man and woman knowingly enter into a temporary marriage under similar circumstances, with both parties agreeing to a specific time interval, then this marriage is deemed to be not legal. Somehow, the jurists have been able to satisfy themselves that the deception involved in this matter is morally superior to duplicity, and that the act of deception on the part of the male carries with it no negative sanction in this life or the next.

※　※

Lewdness

The word lewd is Old English in origin meaning to be un-learned or unprincipled, but it is now generally used to refer to actions or speech that is sexually provocative in an offensive manner. In the Qur'an, the concept of lewdness covers a wide range of sexual indiscretions from adultery to sodomy, with the following verses giving rise to a number of interpretive difficulties.

> If any of your women commit a lewd act, call four witnesses from among you, then, if they testify to their guilt, keep the women at home until death comes to them or until God gives them another way out. If two men commit a lewd act, punish them both; if they repent and mend their ways, leave them alone—God is always ready to accept repentance, He is full of mercy. (4:15-16)

On the face of it, these two verses appear to provide a case of parallelism, in that both refer to the performance of lewd acts, both mention punishment, and both end with a reference to God. The fact that one of these verses concerns women and the other men can be viewed as an example of the equitable treatment of the sexes in the Qur'an. There are, however, important internal differences between these two verses.

In the case of women, four witnesses must testify to their guilt prior to punishment being meted out, while in the case of men no mention of witnesses is made. Again in the case of women, the specific punishment outlined is confinement, while in the case of men no particular form of punishment is recommended. Further, in the case of women, the only release from confinement comes either with death (one would assume by natural causes) or through some other mechanism provided by God. In a note attached to the end of verse 15, Abdel Haleem suggests that a possible way out being referred to is through marriage (2005: 52). However, we might also speculate that, on the basis of the final part of verse 16, repentance would also constitute a legitimate way out.

Turning to alternate translations of these verses, while Yusuf Ali agrees with Abdel Haleem in translating the first part of verse 16 as referring to two men, Arberry uses the phrase, "And when two of you commit indecency," thus introducing ambiguity with respect to both gender identity and the parallel structure. Pickthall goes even further in this respect by rendering the phrase as, "And as for the two of you who are guilty thereof," thereby implying that the verses are to be interpreted as one continuous sequence. Even though the differences introduced by these translators provide no definitive means of determining the nature of the lewd act being referred to, the translations of Abdel Haleem and Yusuf Ali are more consistent with the view that the sexual indiscretions being referred to are between members of the same sex. Conversely, the translations of Arberry and Pickthall are more consistent with what would emerge as the majoritarian perspective among Islamic exegetes and jurists that the indiscretion being referred to is adultery. Unfortunately, there is no way for us to determine the extent to which the interpretive history of these verses influenced the translation process.

If these verses are referring to adultery then we might wonder why this fact is not stated directly, especially when several other references to it can be found throughout the Qur'an, for example, in the following verse where it appears among a list of prohibitions against activities such as infanticide, stealing from orphans, breaking pledges and blindly following something that you know is not true. "And do not go anywhere near adultery: it is an outrage, and an evil path" (17:32). In surah 24, the subject receives extensive coverage, with the appropriate punishment being clearly specified: "Strike the adulteress and the adulterer one hundred times" (24:2).

As Nadia Abu-Zahra points out, proving that a couple had committed adultery on the basis of the criteria laid out in surah four would be extremely difficult, as it is unlikely that there would be four witnesses to the act of sexual intercourse, especially between a couple who would undoubtedly be taking every precaution to avoid detection (2001: 28). On the other hand, surah 24 contains precise regulations with respect to how a husband may bring a charge of adultery against his wife, how a wife is to defend herself against such an accusation, and the punishment that is to be administered to third parties who, in bringing an accusation of adultery against a women, fail to provide four witnesses.

Historically, the majority of commentators have taken the position that the verses in surah 24 abrogate the related verses found in surah 4, thus replacing the punishment of confinement with the punishment of one hundred lashes. Furthermore, based on the existence of a reference to stoning adulterers found in the hadith literature, which contains a declaration by the caliph Umar that there had been a verse in the Qur'an prescribing this form of punishment, but that it had been lost, these same scholars have suggested that the instruction to stone abrogates the punishment of lashing (Stewart 2004: 584). There is certainly a precedent for stoning as a form of capital punishment in Hebrew scripture, but in the Qur'an the few verses that refer to it do so with respect to stones falling from the sky upon God's enemies (Frolov 2006: 130).

Alternately, if these verses are referring to sexual indiscretions between members of the same sex, then we might anticipate that the text would address the matter with specific reference to both men and women, which, according to some translators and exegetes, it appears to do. The manner in which the corresponding punishment is described would seem to reflect an assessment that this behaviour is more a source of embarrassment for the participants than it is a threat to social stability. This is an important point because, in the case of adultery, should it result in pregnancy, the inability to determine paternity would impact the right of a child to inherit. No such risk is attached to same-sex indiscretion. The fact that the text is unclear as to the exact nature of the indiscretion involved is consistent with the fact that same-sex indecency is not discussed explicitly anywhere else in the Qur'an. What is discussed in several locations, however, is the behaviour of the people of Sodom.

> And Lot: when he said to his people, "You practice outrageous acts that no people before you have ever committed. How can you lust after men, waylay travelers, and commit evil in your gatherings?" the only answer his

people gave was, "Bring God's punishment down on us, if what you say is true." (29:28-29)

The references to the story of Lot might be interpreted as a way in which an otherwise taboo topic (i.e., sodomy) can be discussed quite explicitly and yet indirectly, as if, while it is something that other people have done, there is no direct inference that the Arabs hearing the message of the Qur'an are engaged in such activity. As Everett Rowson points out, the only other possible reference to this sort of indecency is with respect to the "everlasting youths" (56:17, 76:19), who serve as cupbearers in Paradise (2002: 445). While the exegetes do not attribute homosexual function to these youths, many works in the Arabic literary tradition have done so.

I would suggest that treating these verses as if they are referring to adultery introduces an unnecessary level of complexity into the text of the Qur'an and its interpretation, especially when the subject of adultery in dealt with so clearly and completely in surah 24.

Wife Beating

Very few verses in the Qur'an have given rise to more discussion, both within Muslim communities and without, than the so-called Beating Verse (4:34), in which it appears that husbands are given permission to hit their wives. I say appears because even though there has been a long tradition, right from the time of the Prophet, of assuming that the content, if not the intent, of this verse is clear, I would suggest that the way in which the verse is written, the way that it is positioned within the text and the history of interpretation of this verse do not adequately support this conclusion. In what follows, I first provide the text of four different translations of the verse, including a discussion of any notes provided by the translator, together with an examination of what might be viewed as a literal reading of these alternate versions. I then provide an analysis of the way in which a number of contemporary scholars have reviewed the history of interpretation of this verse and how they have tried to make sense of this verse in the context of today's world. Finally, I outline an alternate way of approaching the interpretation of this verse that is based in part on recognizing the rhetorical fallacy of the loaded question. Here is the text of the verse from Abdel Haleem's translation:

> Husbands should take good care of their wives, with[a] [the bounties] God has given to some more than others and with what they spend out of their own money. Righteous wives are devout and guard what God would have them guard in their husbands' absence. If you fear high-handedness[b] from your wives, remind them [of the teachings of God], then ignore them when you go to bed, then hit them.[c] If they obey you, then you have no right to act against them: God is most high and great.

At the simplest level, this verse appears to consist of five distinct components that can be described as follows:

- the obligations of husbands towards their wives
- the obligations of wives towards their husbands

- a detailed course of action for dealing with wives under particular circumstances
- a caution against applying the stated course of action when certain conditions exist, and
- a pair of divine names

Addressing the last of these components first, Neal Robinson points out that pairs of divine names are often employed as section breaks within surahs, or as a means of emphasizing the statement that precedes them (2003a: 200). As will be explained in greater detail below, the verse (4:35) that immediately follows the Beating Verse deals with efforts to reconcile marital problems, so it appears in this case that the divine names are not being used to indicate a section break. Rather, they seem to be acting as a conjunction or punctuation mark between discussions of related topics, directing the reader to pause at this point to reflect on what has just been said. In support of this interpretation, the specific divine attributes being referred to (most high, great) might be interpreted as an effort to emphasize that, to the extent that husbands have power over their wives, God's power over men and all of humanity is that much greater, almost as if to say, "so don't forget it the next time you want to discipline your wife."

The initial component of the verse includes the auxiliary verb *should*, potentially implying that the action of caretaking is recommended but not obligatory. Similarly, a particular quality of care is identified, implying that the care provided is to consist of something beyond a basic maintenance level. Combined, these elements might be interpreted to mean that while it is assumed that husbands *will* take care of their wives, just as they had in pre-Islamic times, God intends that they now go beyond this minimal standard and take *good* care of their wives. The two sources that husbands can draw upon to provide this care are God's bounties and what they have of their own wealth. This latter notion seems unproblematic and it is logical to assume that some men will have more wealth than others.

Similarly, while the nature of the bounties is not specified, it is clear that God gives some people more of these than others. However, it is not at all clear whether this statement is suggesting that some men receive more than other men or that men receive more than women. Placing this part of the verse in the context of the directions outlined to this point in the surah, it could be referring back to the subject of inheritance, in which case we know that men are entitled to double what a woman can receive. Alternately, it is reasonable to suggest that, depending on their family circumstances, some women are likely to have more property and wealth than others, and so if a man's wife comes to him with a substantial amount of money, then some of that money should be spent on her, along with whatever amount of his own money he may choose to spend on her.

The second component is interesting in that it uses the adjective *righteous* to modify the subject wives, implying that there are wives who are not righteous. Rather than viewing this construct as an assessment of individual moral character, it may reflect the fact that in this period many men had adopted Islam, but perhaps their wives had not, or maybe did so at a later point than their husbands. The religious status of the wives appears to be questioned further through the use of a tautological element stating that righteous women are devout, again begging the question or suggesting that there are righteous women who are not devout. This component also makes use of veiled language, which could reflect the fact that, even though the meaning and intent of the original Arabic would have been evident at the time the verse was revealed, the translator is reluctant to employ sexually explicit language, or it could mean that the original Arabic is equally vague. In either case, the implication is that the reader will somehow know what is being suggested without the message being explicitly stated. This component is also highly circumstantial, implying that the responsibility for guarding the object being referred to rests with women when their husbands are away from home. Are they not responsible to guard it when their husbands are around? Perhaps the onus is on the husbands to guard it when they are at home, as part of the good quality care that is to be provided.

The third component is at the heart of ongoing controversy around the meaning of this verse and is quite complicated in its structure. The statement begins with a conditional that appears to imply that what follows is not predicated on the actual performance of specific actions by wives, but only on their husbands' fears that certain actions may take place. The action anticipated is referred to as high-handedness, which could be interpreted to mean acting in a superior manner. It is not clear, however, whether this superiority is grounded in material wealth, moral integrity, kinship or any other specific criterion, nor is it clear whether this superiority is directed toward the husband, the broader community or Islam.

While it might be plausible to imagine a wife at times acting in an overbearing manner toward her husband, based on any number of factors, one of which might be the fact that she has more money than he does or because she comes from a more prestigious family, it is not unreasonable to suggest that she might just as easily act that way out of the conviction that the beliefs and practices of her kin and predecessors are just as good as, or even superior to, what was now being advocated by the Prophet. Irrespective of the origin of the behaviour, the three steps that can be taken in response to the suspicion of high-handedness are presented in a sequential manner that appears to imply that the first step should be tried first, and if it does not produce the desired results then the second step should be tried, with the third step only being employed as a last resort. This interpretation is supported by the fact that each punishment is incrementally more severe than its predecessor. The bracketed text appended to the first step appears to suggest that at first a husband is to remind his wife of God's teachings about the relationship between husbands and wives. As a second step, a husband is to show no affection towards his wife when they are alone together, most likely implying that he is to abstain from having sexual relations with her. The final instruction to hit appears unambiguous, but even a conservative reading of this instruction would suggest that this is a last resort.

The fourth component (if they obey you...) might appear to be the most straightforward statement in the verse, but even it gives rise to an interesting question. Is the reference to obedience to be interpreted as applying more generally or just with respect to this particular matter? If the latter, then the conditional helps to reinforce the graded interpretation of the punishments, suggesting that, if following the act of being reminded, the inappropriate behaviour ceases, then the husband has no right to move on to the next step, or otherwise take action against his wife. If, on the other hand, a wife is to obey her husband in all things, can we conclude from this that the punishments listed here are limited to a specific type of disobedience? Are there punishments for other types of disobedience?

Abdel Haleem attaches three footnotes (superscripts a, b and c) to this verse (2005: 54). In the first note he remarks that the word *with* should be understood instrumentally rather than causally; that is, suggesting *by means of* rather than *because of*. In other words, husbands are to care for their wives by means of the bounties they have received, not because they have received those bounties. He uses the second note to refer the reader to a parallel verse that appears later in the surah (4:128) where the notion of high-handedness (assuming superiority over your spouse) is used with respect to the behaviour of husbands rather than wives. His intention with this note is unclear, but could be interpreted to suggest that he wants to emphasize that high-handedness is not solely within the behavioural repertoire of wives. At the same time, however, it draws attention to the fact that the mention of high-handedness on the part of husbands gives rise to a discussion of reconciliation, rather than punishment. In the final note, directing the reader to a more thorough discussion of the matter in one of his earlier books, Abdel Haleem points out that, based on the circumstances of revelation of this verse, the permission to hit refers to delivering a single blow (1999: 53). More details of his analysis appear below.

Here is the text of the verse, as translated by Yusuf Ali (2004):

(Husbands) are the protectors[545]
And maintainers of their (wives)
Because Allah has given
The one more (strength)
Than the other, and because
They support them
From their means.
Therefore the righteous women
Are devoutly obedient, and guard
In (the husband's) absence
What Allah would have them guard.[546]
As to those women
On whose part ye fear
Disloyalty and ill-conduct,
Admonish them (first),[547]
(Next), refuse to share their beds,
(And last) spank them (lightly);[547A]
But if they return to obedience,
Seek not against them[548]
Means (of annoyance):
For Allah is Most High,
Great (above you all).

This translation predates that of Abdel Haleem by more than 60 years (c. 1938), and so it reflects not only a particular style of English usage, but also likely reflects a view of morality and gender relations consistent with that time.

In the first component of the verse, the concept of care-taking is divided into two aspects, protection and maintenance, both of which are impersonal in tone and sound more like broader social rather than marital obligations. In contrast to the instrumental interpretation offered by Abdel Haleem, Yusuf Ali offers a causal interpretation that has two components, the first being strength and the second being wealth. So, rather than answering the question of how husbands are to provide for their wives, Yusuf Ali interprets this component from the perspective of why, linking the concept of strength to the process of protection and the concept of wealth, or means, to the process of maintenance. Husbands protect their wives because they are stronger and husbands maintain their wives because they have the means to do so. While it would be easy to assume, on the basis of his use of the word protection, that Yusuf Ali is implying physical strength, it is not unreasonable to suggest that he might be referring to moral or religious strength.

The only significant difference in this translation of the second component is that the concept of devotion is more directly linked to the idea of obedience. The pairing of the expressions "righteous women" and "devoutly obedient" might be interpreted to suggest that while women were obedient to their husbands in pre-Islamic times, as a means of securing their material well-being, with the advent of Islam their obedience is more directly linked to their spiritual well-being.

102

This translation of the initial aspect of the third component is interesting in that the potential transgression (high-handedness) is defined more specifically as disloyalty and ill conduct. As with the concepts of protection and maintenance, these actions sound more social than personal in nature. While the notion of disloyalty could be interpreted to mean marital infidelity, it could just as easily be associated with the act of turning away from, or speaking out against, Islam. The same sort of reasoning applies to the notion of ill conduct, which might suggest any sort of behaviour that the community would deem to be inappropriate, but might be more specifically referring to actions that could be interpreted as inconsistent with Islam. With respect to the second aspect of this component, Yusuf Ali parenthetically makes explicit the graded nature of these punishments, even going so far as to doubly soften the idea of hitting through the use of the verb *spank*, an obvious allusion to the controlled and largely symbolic physical correction of a misbehaving child, and the tempering of even this minimal act with the adverb lightly.

The fourth component contains a significant difference, in that, by using the word "return," it assumes that an act of disobedience has taken place, some level of punishment has been meted out, and that husbands are to seek no further action against their wives. The idea that the punishments are interpreted as annoyances might suggest that, even though a three-step regimen of punishment is laid out in the Qur'an, Yusuf Ali is of the opinion that the text implies that it is only rarely that a reprimand would not suffice.

Regarding the use of the divine names, the parenthetical addition of the expression "above you all," might be viewed as a cautionary note to husbands who may perceive that they are superior to their wives.

Yusuf Ali provides five footnotes (superscripts 545, 546, 547, 547A and 548) to this verse (2004: 195). In the first note, he suggests that the concept of protection is being used in a business sense to imply taking care of, or managing your own affairs or the affairs of others. The second note explains that, in her husband's absence, a wife guards her own virtue as well as the reputation and property of her husband. The third note indicates that the punishments are to be administered in order, adding that in the opinion of the jurists, should it be necessary, it is permissible but not recommended to use a "slight physical correction." Yusuf Ali goes on to suggest that the interpretation of this verse is directly linked to the interpretation of the next verse (4:35), which recommends that members of the extended family are to act as arbitrators. He views the two verses together as outlining a four-step process designed to maintain harmonious marriages.

The fourth note, which interestingly appears for the first time in the most recent edition of this translation (2004, the previous edition was 1999), likely reflects the response of the present editorial board at Amana Publications to the increased scholarly and public attention being received by this verse. Specifically, the editors point out that there are at least seventeen different ways to understand the Arabic word commonly being translated as hit, including the notions of avoid, leave, separate and travel, or to stay away from, all apparently directed at helping a wife realize what life would be like should a divorce ensue. The fifth note emphasizes the need for forgiveness and the fact that to continue to express anger, to nag or to speak sarcastically is contrary to what God wills for humanity.

This third translation by Alan Jones (2007) introduces a few significant changes from the prior two examples. Husbands and wives become men and women, suggesting that irrespective of the bonds of marriage the relative positions and obligations of men and women remain constant. In this respect, the use of the word "overseer" carries with it connotations of command and control. Further, high-handedness or ill conduct becomes rebelliousness, suggesting either failure to comply, or at least protest against whatever standards women are being asked to comply with. Additionally, the obligation of women is expressed in terms of what God has done for them, rather than being expressed with reference to their husbands, or men.

> Men are overseers of women
> because God has granted some of them bounty
> in preference to others and because of the possessions
> which they spend.
> Righteous women are obedient,
> guarding the invisible
> because God has guarded [them].
> Admonish[p] those women whose rebelliousness you fear,
> shun them in [their] resting-places
> and hit them.
> If they obey you, do not seek a [further] way against them.
> God is Exalted and Great.

With the superscript "p" inserted after the word admonish, Jones is indicating that this use of the imperative form of the verb is given in the plural. He does not suggest how the plural should be interpreted, but here are a couple of alternatives. First, this use of the plural could simply be a matter of maintaining grammatical consistency, given that the verse is addressed to any and all men who might find themselves in this situation. Second, looking forward to the advice on the role of the family in settling domestic woes outlined in the next verse (4:35), the plural might be interpreted as suggesting that other members of the family should also engage in chastising and correcting the behaviour of a rebellious wife. The use of the parenthetical "their" to modify resting-places suggests a completely different interpretation from those of Abdel Haleem or Yusuf Ali. What Jones appears to be suggesting is that women be sent to their own room. In situations where a man has more than one wife, it is logical to assume that each wife would have her own sleeping quarters, and that in administering this punishment the husband would not come to them, thus isolating them from intimate contact altogether. Unlike Yusuf Ali, Jones makes no effort to avoid or soften the instruction to hit, almost appearing to suggest that these punishments are to be employed in conjunction with each other.

In providing a fourth version of the verse, from the so-called reformist translation produced collaboratively under the principle editorship of Turkish scholar Edip Yuksel (2007), my intention is to demonstrate that some translators have gone to the extent of eliminating any reference to beating altogether.

> The men are to support the women by
> what God has gifted them over one

another and for what they spend of their money. The reformed women are devotees and protectors of privacy what God has protected. As for those women from whom you fear disloyalty, then you shall advise them, abandon them in the bedchamber, and separate them; if they obey you, then do not seek a way over them; God is High, Great.

Even though this new translation is designed to correct previous biases and to more accurately reflect the original and ongoing intent of the text, it is not particularly clear. Who are the reformed women? The ones who have embraced Islam? Is disloyalty to be viewed as adultery, failure to follow the dictates of their husbands, or failure to abide by the dictates of God? One of the problems with this sort of translation, especially with consideration to those who are just beginning to explore the Qur'an, and who might be looking for the scriptural origins of particular issues, is that it conveniently glosses over a fourteen-hundred-year history of debate over whether in fact the Qur'an gives permission for a husband to hit his wife.

Before moving on to an examination of the way in which this verse has been interpreted by exegetes, it is important to reiterate the fact that the art/science of translation is already a critical and tremendously complex process of interpretation in its own right. At the same time, given the scope of differences we have observed in the four translations of this single verse, it is difficult to defend the proposition that a thorough understanding of the Arabic language is a necessary or sufficient prerequisite for the study of the Qur'an. Reading the Qur'an in Arabic is neither a means of avoiding the interpretive hazards of translation, nor is it a more direct avenue to understanding the text. Further, as evidenced by the notes and parenthetical insertions of the translators, it should be abundantly clear that a non-historical or decontextualized reading of the Qur'an is doomed to be an incorrect one.

WITH RESPECT to exegetical interpretations, Abdel Haleem observes that efforts to understand this verse have too often been informed by male chauvinism, outdated prejudices and media sensationalism (1999: 46-47). Putting these biases aside, he suggests that the foundations for a legitimate interpretation are to be found in a linguistic analysis of the text, Muhammad's own interpretation of the verse and what the Qur'an has to say about marital difficulties in other verses. Among the correctives he offers are, that the verse refers specifically to husbands and wives and not to men and women more generally, that the role of husbands with respect to their wives and families is one of stewardship and that, as reinforced in 4:35, reconciliation is the goal of any acts of correction or intervention.

Hadia Mubarak attempts a contemporary reinterpretation of the verse through the application of what she describes as valid hermeneutical principles, namely, an intratextual reading of the Qur'an, the evidence found in the authentic hadith literature, the circumstances of revelation, the aim (*maqsad*) of the verse and grammatical considerations (2004: 265). She begins by pointing out that the application of valid interpretive processes has been inhibited by the retrospective canonization of classical and medieval interpretations, which have not only acquired the inappropriate and un-Islamic attribution of infallibility reserved for the Qur'an, but also reflect the view that interpretive authority is somehow directly proportional to the exegete's temporal proximity to the Prophet. One of the consequences of this development is that people are critical of the Qur'an for giving permission for husbands to beat their wives, when in fact it is the interpretations that have done so. As she says, "it is the interpretive process, not the Revelation itself, that is open to critique and historicization" (2004: 266).

Mubarak explains that the problem begins with al-Tabari (d. 923), who interpreted the initial aspect of the first component of the verse to mean that men have legal authority over women, and thus the right to discipline them, and the second aspect to mean that God gives more to men than to women (2004: 269). This interpretation takes on the status of an a priori assumption in later interpretations, culminating in the work of Ibn Kathir (d. 1371), who holds that men are to lead, discipline and preside over their wives, thus extending the ambit of male authority from the domestic to the political realm, all based on a weak Prophetic tradition which states that a people ruled by a woman would never succeed (2004: 270). Perhaps as a reflection of the dominance of misogynistic interpretations of the Qur'an, but certainly as a demonstration of the extremes to which interpretive reductionism can go, Ibn Kathir suggests that the meaning of disloyalty or high-handedness in this verse refers specifically to the wife's refusal to have sexual intercourse with her husband (2004: 273).

As for her own analysis, Mubarak indicates that, while the hadith literature and circumstances of revelation are not much help with respect to understanding this verse, an intratextual reading of the Qur'an clearly indicates that men and women are considered to be ontological equals, as stated in the opening verse of the fourth surah discussed earlier in this chapter, and that men and women share moral responsibility to promote justice (9:51). Further, when the Beating Verse is read along with the verse that follows it (4:35), it should be clear that the aim of this sequence can only be interpreted as being directed toward reconciliation, and that "any reading of the Qur'an that promotes or sanctions domestic abuse would violate the Qur'anic paradigm of marital relations" (2004: 275).

Mubarak concludes that any interpretation of this verse which suggests that men are allowed to beat their wives is inconsistent with the Qur'anic precepts of "ordaining justice and establishing tranquility as the basis of marriage," and that if the directive is to be interpreted as meaning to hit, then such an interpretation must be understood "in a restrictive rather than a prescriptive sense" (2004: 285). Speaking more broadly about contemporary efforts to understand the Qur'an, Mubarak argues that,

> without a process of reinterpretation, one reduces the
> Qur'an to a historical text that loses any sense of rel-

evance or applicability to the societal setting in which it is being read and to the people for whom it was revealed. (2004: 287)

Karen Bauer presents a somewhat different perspective on the history of interpretation of this verse, suggesting that,

pre-modern and modern exegetes have a common method of selectively drawing on sources and precedents: they work with their heritage in order to forge interpretations that, on the one hand, preserve continuity with the past, and on the other, are relevant to their particular milieu. (2006: 130)

She suggests that a major shift in interpretation took place as a result of the influence of the work of Ibn al-Arabi (d. 1148), who suggested that men are superior to women in two ways—perfection in rationality and perfection in religion—based on an authentic hadith found in the collection by Bukhari which states:

This is what the Prophet clarified when he said: "I haven't seen people more deficient in reason and religion, who can go straight to the hearts of upright men, than you women." (qtd. in Bauer 2006: 132)

The premise of women's deficient rationality became the primary foundation for the establishment of more restrictive understandings of the status and role of women (133). Bauer cautions that, even though this premise may sound misogynistic to modern ears, there is no clear indication that pre-modern exegetes saw it as reflecting anything more than the natural order of things (134). In this regard, Bauer draws attention to the seemingly contradictory position advocated by the majority of legal scholars that, while women can offer opinions on the law (i.e., act as *muftis*), they cannot serve as judges. This position is counterintuitive, because, as she expresses it,

> a *mufti* forms legal opinions using independent reasoning, whereas a judge enacts those legal opinions in the settling of disputes; the post of *mufti* requires a higher order of mental reasoning than that of a judge. (2006: 135)

Looking at the situation in Syria at present, Bauer examines the differences between how reformist cleric Muhammad al-Habash, who advocates that men and women are equal partners, and conservative cleric Said al-Buti, who continues to hold the view that women are rationally deficient, interpret the notion of men's authority over women. In support of the conservative view, which Bauer finds to represent the majority position among Syrian clerics, justifications are offered that refer to women's emotions and natural differences between the sexes, to the extent that, according to some clerics, while women are permitted to serve as expert witnesses in court, they cannot do so in murder cases because the horror will overwhelm them (2006: 136). Even among the more liberal clerics, who suggest that the rational deficiency argument does not make sense, more leeway is provided for women to participate in the public sphere, but their roles at home are still seen to reflect more traditional values.

In her contribution to understanding historical developments in the interpretation of this verse, Kecia Ali examines the apparent inconsistency between the methodological principles that al-Shafi'i (d. 820) outlines in his more theoretical work *Risalah* and his application of those principles in his *Kitab al-Umm* (2006). Ali points out that while al-Shafi'i is generally understood to have recognized four sources for the establishment of law—the Qur'an, the sunnah, analogy and consensus—as discussed in the previous chapter, Joseph Lowry (2004) suggests that, for al-Shafi'i, clear guidance (*bayan*) from a revealed source always takes precedence (2006: 144). While the Beating Verse is not discussed in the *Risalah*, in the *Kitab al-Umm* an alternate mechanism for dealing with wifely high-handedness is mentioned, with no revelatory precedent offered in support. While primarily relying on a hadith that states, "the best of you will not strike," to frame his opinion on hitting, al-Shafi'i introduces a transactional view of marriage to suggest that disloyalty can lead to a loss of maintenance (149-50). As Ali points out, this view reflects a more legalistic rather than exegetical approach to interpreting the verse, which is based on the idea that in exchange for maintenance a women offers herself as a sexual partner to her husband (150). The precise link between a loss of maintenance and hitting is not established, nor is any justification provided for invoking a non-revelatory source of interpretation. Ali does not push for a strong conclusion from her analysis, but she does appear to suggest that instances may arise where a more practical and legalistic interpretation of the Qur'an takes precedence over theological concerns. We might also observe from this analysis that, even within a couple of centuries of the death of the Prophet, interpreting the Beating Verse presented a daunting challenge to the integrity of the Qur'an and to the development of systematic theological and legal principles within Islam.

Ayesha Chaudhry reviews the efforts of some contemporary believing scholars to interpret the Beating Verse in a way that reconciles their ideas on justice and gender equality with their acceptance of the Qur'an as the literal word of God (2006). She divides the range of methodological approaches into three basic categories that reflect the way that scholars differentially privilege the text of the Qur'an, tradition and contemporary social reality. In her view, traditionalists accept the primacy of the Qur'an and allow tradition to trump contemporary concerns. Among the advocates of this position, Chaudhry points out that, while accepting the instruction to hit, Jamal Badawi sees this as largely symbolic, while Ahmed Shafaat suggests that the action must be an "energetic demonstration of the anger, frustration and love of the husband" (qtd. in Chaudhry 2006: 160). Idealists still accept the primacy of the Qur'an but suggest that it is the exegetes who introduced patriarchal and misogynistic interpretations of the text. However, in their efforts to adhere to their ideals, scholars such as Asma Barlas and Hadia Mubarak are selective in their use of tradition, reversing their own position and choosing in the case of 4:34 to privilege the more egalitarian interpretations associated with Prophetic tradition over what is written in the Qur'an. The reformist position gives greater weight to contemporary social concerns, with some scholars going so far as to suggest that interpreters must "consciously depart from the letter of the text" (qtd. in Chaudhry 2006: 163). For her part, Chaudhry advocates a middle way that is not bound by textual or contextual fundamentalism (165).

In a very brief but highly insightful article, Laury Silvers uses the thought of Ibn al-Arabi (d. 1240) to explore the problem created by the mere existence of the Beating Verse (2006). Based on the premise from al-Arabi that, while God intends all meanings that can be derived from the text of the Qur'an, God does not necessarily approve of all meanings, Silvers suggests that ethical freedom is part of the burden that humans accepted from God, as stated in the following verse:

> We offered the Trust to the heavens, the earth, and the mountains, yet they refused to undertake it and were afraid of it; mankind undertook it—they have always been inept and foolish. (33:72)

Comparing the struggle to fight our baser instincts and make good choices in life to the rebellious acts that children engage in as part of healthy psychological growth, she states:

> We may have the ability and right to decide not to eat our vegetables, but we also have obligations to God, our bodies and our loved ones. Inasmuch as we deny those rights and obligations in their proper scope, we use these qualities to our own selfish ends. (2006: 175)

She goes on to stress that the conflicted response given by the Prophet to the revelation of the Beating Verse, as reflected in the fact that, according to tradition, he not only spoke out against hitting but was also uncomfortable even reciting this verse, demonstrates the "perfection of his humanity" (176). Silvers concludes that the purpose for the very existence of the verse is to present a crisis of conscience that will lead us to reject beating. Referring to Muhammad's recognition of his own place in the world, she warns that, "we would be terrified if we knew the extraordinary extent of our responsibility in being human" (178).

Mohamed Mahmoud reviews the interpretive efforts of a number of classical commentators, pointing out that by giving preference to the Prophetic tradition associated with the application of this verse, as opposed to more literally following what was revealed, scholars and jurists have chosen to introduce a sort of "virtual abrogation" or "abrogative suspension" of the instruction to hit (2006). While recognizing the dilemma of appearing to reject the dictates of the Qur'an on ethical grounds, Mahmoud makes the larger point that, adopting this approach with respect to 4:34, establishes the precedent for virtual abrogation to serve as a hermeneutic tool in the further development of Islamic tradition more generally (2006: 550).

Rachel Scott examines the efforts of three contemporary scholars, Fatima Mernissi, Muhammad al-Talbi and Amina Wadud, to take a contextualist approach to understanding why the Qur'an permits husbands to beat their wives (2009). Mernissi suggests that the Beating Verse was revealed at the same time as the Hijab Verse (33:53), an unstable period during which military and political considerations led to a re-establishment of male supremacy in Islamic society. Observing that Mernissi seems to be suggesting that in revealing these verses, "God was more pragmatic than his more idealistic Prophet," Scott wonders why God would not have sent down another verse after the period of instability was over (2009: 68). Al-Talbi's approach is similar in that he argues that verses must be understood in light of the historical and social circumstances in which they were revealed, leading him to the conclusion that 4:34 was revealed as a means of strengthening the community (70). Suggesting that Wadud's methodology is more sophisticated and systematic than that of Mernissi or al-Talbi, Scott points out that, even though she would come to take a more cautious attitude about the objectivity of her own position, Wadud interprets this verse as placing severe restrictions on existing practice, rather than giving permission for a new practice (hitting) to be carried out (74). Scott goes on to point out some of the problems with a contextualist approach to understanding the Qur'an, especially with respect to the hazard of textual or methodological relativism, concluding that there is a moral responsibility attached to one's interpretive choices, no matter what they may be (80).

AS OBSERVED with the various efforts to translate this verse, the historical and contemporary exegetical interpretations just discussed display a range of approaches and opinions that raise as many questions as they provide answers. While we do not appear to be anywhere near reaching a consensus as to the purpose and meaning of this verse, there is no question that we remain troubled not only by its existence, but also by some of the ways in which it has been understood and applied. In what follows, I outline two interpretive mechanisms that can help us in our quest to establish a level of comfort with the Beating Verse and the social issues it raises. First, I introduce the logical fallacy of the loaded question, which is often employed as a rhetorical strategy when attempting to determine guilt or innocence in legal matters, as a means of gaining a better understanding of the original context in which this verse was revealed, as well as providing a way to better articulate the hazard of confusing historical and contemporary standards. Second, I examine the co-text of the Beating Verse, in order to demonstrate how other textual elements within the fourth surah provide significant clues with respect to how to perform an internally consistent exegesis.

Most people will be familiar with the fallacy of the loaded question, from the following common example: "When did you stop beating your wife?" (Walton 1999). Such questions constitute a form of entrapment, artificially limiting a respondent's ability to provide a correct answer without simultaneously putting forth an admission of guilt. In terms of the exegetical principles we have been discussing, a loaded question presupposes the context within which to understand the text under consideration. In this case the context is one in which a husband is beating his wife and the text records the effort to establish whether this behaviour is still being carried out. On the face of it, this is not a moral question; it is simply an attempt to establish the facts. However, an important aspect of this loaded question resides in the fact that the questioner is relying on the implicit evaluative nature of the question to elicit a certain effect among those hearing the response. As Walton points out, even asking this question today constitutes a highly prejudicial attack on a respondent, because spousal abuse is viewed as morally reprehensible, and those who commit it are highly stigmatized (1999: 383).

Relating these ideas to the interpretation of the Beating Verse, when presented with the question of whether the Qur'an gives permission for a husband to beat his wife, it appears that we must answer in the affirmative—the verse does exist. However, is this a form of entrapment? By asking the question in what appears to be a straightforward logical manner, are we in fact allowing an unproven assumption to contextualize our response, and are we accepting an evaluative framework that inevitably leaves us with an unpalatable moral conundrum? In an effort to maintain what we might assume to be the moral consistency of the Qur'an, do we have to play one part of the text off against another, or even go the extent of rejecting one part of the text altogether? Perhaps, we are asking the wrong question.

There is no way for us to determine with any level of certainty the extent to which wife-beating was carried out among pre-Islamic Arabs, and we have no idea of the extent to which such activity may or may not have met with social approval. The fact that several verses in the Qur'an appear to be advocating for greater equality between men and women combined with the fact that the Beating Verse exists at all would seem to suggest that, whatever the views on this behaviour might have been up to the point of the revelation of this verse, a re-examination of the issue was now being presented. Consequently, care must be taken not to transfer contemporary cultural, legal, moral and social perspectives back fourteen centuries in an effort to condone or condemn the content or context of the Qur'an.

Framing the whole matter differently, we might view the interpretive task as one of trying to determine the nature of the question to which verse 4:34 is the answer. Avoiding the fallacy of the loaded question, and acknowledging both the difference in the moral climate of the time and the intention of the Qur'an to provide a new moral framework for the Arab people, the proper (unloaded) question might be: "What are the circumstances under which a man may still beat his wife?"

In an effort to answer this contemporary question, the Beating Verse needs to be read in light of the statements surrounding it, as well as with respect to parallel thematic and structural elements within the rest of the surah. The specific elements to be considered include the parallel sequence contained in 4:3, the discussion of wealth and God's bounty in 4:32-33, the advocacy of reconciliation in 4:35 and the mention of high-handedness in 4:128.

In the sources that I have examined, I have yet to find an adequate or even cursory coverage of the meaning of the conditional phrase "if you fear" that precedes the mention of high-handedness in 4:34. On one level this phrase appears to be suggesting that high-handedness does not in fact have to have occurred prior to a husband inflicting punishment on his wife—he only has to fear that it might occur. I would suggest that one way to understand this phrase on its own terms is to view it as a recognition, or acknowledgment, of the difficulty associated with the adoption of the new standards contained in the message of the Qur'an. In other words, it might be a shortened version of: "If you fear that in dealing with the exigencies of everyday life, in accordance with the precepts now being presented to you as a Muslim, you will encounter too much opposition or insurmountable difficulties...." While this interpretation might be viewed as highly speculative, the fact remains that the purpose and meaning of this phrase are significantly understudied. For now I am primarily concerned with the rhetorical use of the phrase, "If you fear."

The principle clue to understanding how this phrase is being used can be found not only in the fact that it occurs again in the next verse (4:35), discussed below, but that a parallel structural and thematic element occurs at the beginning of the surah, in 4:3, which was discussed above in the section on marriage. In 4:3, the phrase "if you fear" is used twice, first to introduce a permitted action (marrying up to four wives), and second to suggest that a more advisable course of action is to marry only one. Extending the parallelism to the Beating Verse, the initial use of the phrase again introduces a permitted action (wife-beating), leaving the reader to anticipate that there will be a second use of the phrase to introduce a more advisable course of action. Ignoring the existence and relatedness of 4:35, in trying to understand the Beating Verse, does a great injustice to the internal logic of the Qur'an, especially when such an obvious parallel is employed to deal with another highly controversial topic.

By examining the two verses that precede the Beating Verse, we gain some insight into the meaning of its initial components:

> Do not covet what God has given to some of you more than others—men have the portion they have earned; and women the portion they have earned—you should

rather ask God for some of His bounty: He has full
knowledge of everything. We have appointed heirs for
everything that parents and close relatives leave behind,
including those to whom you have pledged your hands
[in marriage], so give them their share: God is witness to
everything. (4:32-33)

Not only do these verses provide a reminder that the
ongoing discussions in the surah are to be understood
within the broader context of instructions pertaining to
inheritance, they also help us to understand the relationship between wealth and bounty that has caused problems
in interpreting the initial components of 4:34. These verses
suggest that men and women have earned what God has allowed them to earn, and that any differences that may obtain between what any particular man or woman possesses
should not become the basis for covetousness. Instead of
seeking the wealth of others, people are advised to seek
bounty from God, as all wealth, even that which people
appear to have earned on their own, comes from God.

Just as the text of 4:32-33 contains parallel subject matter to the initial portion of 4:34, 4:35 demonstrates both thematic and structural parallelism with the middle part of 4:34:

If you [believers] fear that a couple may break up, appoint
one arbiter from his family and one from hers. Then,
if the couple wants to put things right, God will bring
about a reconciliation between them: He is all knowing,
all aware. (4:35)

Returning to the parallel sequence in 4:3, when this
verse is read along with the Beating Verse, the reader is

provided with the anticipated counterpart to the initial use of "if you fear," and, as in the earlier use of the pairing, a more advisable course of action (reconciliation) is presented. It is difficult to imagine any interpretation of the Beating Verse that would not take account of this obvious, and I would suggest intentional, parallelism.

There is one further structural element that assists in pointing to an appropriate interpretation of 4:34, and that is the mention of high-handedness in 4:128.

> If a wife fears high-handedness or alienation from her husband, neither of them will be blamed if they come to a peaceful settlement, for peace is best. Although human souls are prone to selfishness, if you do good and are mindful of God, He is well aware of all that you do. (4:128)

This verse stands out not only because it reverses the roles of husband and wife, when compared to 4:34, but it also couples alienation (the second prescribed punishment from 4:34) with high-handedness. Remembering Zahniser's suggestion that position is hermeneutic, bringing together the combined sequence of 4:34 and 4:35 with 4:128, an interesting pattern emerges. Initially, wives are the potential perpetrators and husbands are allowed to inflict punishment. In the second phases, both husbands and wives are viewed as the potential source of problems, and in the third instance it is husbands who are singled out as the perpetrators, both for an act similar to what was originally mentioned as an undesirable act and for an act originally associated with a legitimate form of punishment. Thus, the sequence serves to balance the number of times that husbands and wives are mentioned and the attribution of ill-conduct. Further, reconciliation is stated as the appropriate goal and course of action in two instances, in contrast to the single mention of punishment.

Perhaps the major stumbling block for contemporary interpretation is the ethical dilemma presented by the mere existence of the Beating Verse, especially in a world characterized by such a broad spectrum of women's rights regimes. At the same time, the inertia of tradition with respect to understanding and practice is extremely difficult to overcome, and the opinions of scholars rarely trump the dictates of political leaders or charismatic militants. By introducing the fallacy of the loaded question and demonstrating how a co-textual examination of the Beating Verse greatly expands the interpretive possibilities, I hope I have been able to convince readers to at least raise a cautionary note the next time they are asked if, or told that, the Qur'an permits a husband to beat his wife.

Hijab

John Bowen opens his *Why the French Don't Like Headscarves* with the following observation:

> In early 2004, the French government passed a law prohibiting from public schools any clothing that clearly indicated a pupil's religious affiliation. Although worded in a religion-neutral way, everyone understood the law to be aimed at keeping Muslim girls from wearing headscarves in school. (2008: 1)

While the subject of wife beating discussed in the previous section might be viewed as representing a covert activity that is only to be discussed in private, if at all, the issue of veiling is very much a part of public discourse, if for no other reason than it constitutes an overt and increasingly more visible display of religious affiliation. As Cumper and Lewis observe, the hijab commands a great deal of attention in contemporary European and North America societies because it is associated with the appearance of the oppression of young girls and women, it symbolizes the excesses of totalitarian theocracies and it continues to fuel debates over the role of faith in public life (2009: 602-03). Furthermore, the Muslim veil has also acquired iconic status, being used in advertizing to sell everything from cigarettes to toothpaste, and being appropriated as a tool of politics, militarism and eroticism (Shirazi 2001).

In contrast to the ongoing re-examination of the matter of wife beating through efforts to understand how verse 4:34 should be interpreted, developing an understanding of veiling is much more tied to social scientific analyses because of its continued widespread practice within Islam and as a consequence of Islam's encounter with other religious groups and other cultural, political and social norms as Muslim communities are established in various countries throughout the world. However, as with wife beating, the practice of veiling is rooted in the text of the Qur'an, although in a far less literal manner than many might think.

Stowasser points out that the word hijab appears seven times in the Qur'an to indicate spatial or visual separation, or sometimes both (1997: 88). For example, it is used with reference to Mary seeking seclusion from her family in preparation for the birth of Jesus (19:17). It is used to describe the barrier that is placed between the Prophet and the unbelievers in the hereafter (17:45), and it is used with respect to the unbelievers to suggest that their hearts are veiled such that they cannot receive the message of Islam (41:5). The most relevant, and thus most controversial, use of the term is in the so-called Hijab Verse, where it clearly refers to a curtain or partition used to separate the wives of the Prophet from unrelated male visitors.

> Believers, do not enter the Prophet's apartments for a
> meal unless you are given permission to do so; do not
> linger until [a meal] is ready. When you are invited, go
> in; then, when you have taken your meal, leave. Do
> not stay on and talk, for that would offend the Prophet,
> though he would shrink from asking you to leave. God
> does not shrink from the truth. When you ask his wives
> for something, do so from behind a screen: this is purer
> both for your hearts and for theirs. It is not right for
> you to offend God's Messenger, just as you should never
> marry his wives after him: that would be grievous in
> God's eyes. (33:53)

The primary focus of this verse is on behaviours that might offend the Prophet while visiting him in the home of one of his wives. Visitors are instructed not to be overly familiar with his wives, as this might not only offend him, it might also lead to inappropriate desires, with visitors ultimately being warned against the potential of marrying one of the Prophet's wives after he is gone. It is unclear in this instance whether the wives would be desirable in their own right or whether their appeal would be a function of the fact that they had been married to the Prophet. In any case, visitors (the content suggests men) are to speak to the wives of the Prophet from a behind a screen—they are to be visually separated. While the custom of referring to the veil as hijab derives from this verse, the broader concept of veiling incorporates elements of at least two other verses, the first of which is known as the Mantle Verse.

> Prophet, tell your wives, your daughters, and women believers to make their outer garments hang low over them so as to be recognized and not insulted: God is most forgiving, most merciful. (33:59)

This verse shifts the setting away from a private home to being out in public. The implication appears to be that if women allow their garments to hang low, thus concealing their inner garments, their bare legs and more generally their overall shape, they will be respected and recognized as Muslims. So, it appears to be quite clear that wearing concealing clothing is part of a Muslim woman's identity; however, there is no specific reference to covering the head. Further, the recommendation applies to the Prophet's wives, his daughters and to all believing women. The fact that these three groups are specifically mentioned might suggest that there were some who thought, based on the precedent of the Hijab Verse, that this manner of dress was appropriate only for the Prophet's wives. The third relevant verse is the Modesty Verse.

> And tell believing women that they should lower their glances, guard their private parts, and not display their

charms except to their husbands, their fathers, their
husbands' fathers, their sons, their husbands' sons, their
brothers, their brothers' sons, their sisters' sons, their
womenfolk, their slaves, such men as attend them who
have no sexual desire, or children who are not yet aware
of women's nakedness; they should not stamp their feet
so as to draw attention to any hidden charms. (24:31)

The primary content of this verse deals with outlining
those categories of people from whom a woman is not required to conceal herself, and thus can be interpreted to
suggest that she must conceal herself from all others. In
addition to concealment, the final phrase instructs women
not to engage in any movements that will draw attention to
their bodies. The initial phrase is particularly interesting
in that it provides a direct parallel to the preceding verse:
"[Prophet], tell believing men to lower their glances and
guard their private parts: that is purer for them" (24:30).
At the very least this latter verse suggests that the requirement for modest behaviour applies equally to men and
women.

While there can be little argument that these verses
suggest that women must dress modestly, and that they
are to have limited contact with males who are not members of their family, it is a stretch to suggest that the practice of having women cover their heads or their faces has
a firm basis in the Qur'an. Rather, the key to understanding how this practice, and its numerous variations, developed, can be found in the cultural histories of the various
peoples that adopted Islam and in the ways that they man-
aged assimilation. As Stowasser explains, in some cases,

exegetes went so far as to suggest that even a woman's face and hands must be covered because any exposed part of a woman's body is an extension of her genitals and thus must be hidden from view (1997: 101-03).

Abou El Fadl reports on several rulings emerging from questions posed to the Permanent Council for Scientific Research and Legal Opinions (CRLO), the official source of legal rulings in Saudi Arabia (2001: 177-78). Responding to the question of whether it is permissible for women to wear brassieres, the CRLO indicates that in those instances where women are wearing the garment to emphasize their cleavage, or to look like virgins, then they are clearly prohibited from doing so on the basis that wearing such garments amounts to fraud and misrepresentation. If, on the other hand, the garments are being worn for health reasons, then it is permitted. The CRLO similarly ruled against the wearing of high heels which among other things alter the height of the person wearing them and thus contribute to misrepresentation.

As a clear statement of the fact that the misplaced attention on the veil actually masks what really matters, Jennifer Heath states that:

> Neither legislation nor bombing will "solve" veiling. The veil does not need to be solved. The energy that has been expended on veiling, unveiling, reveiling, or deveiling by non-Muslims and Muslims alike has by now become downright preposterous and dangerous. Considering the real problems facing women, ideological battles about the veil are tragic wastes of time. (2008: 320)

War

Introduction

Whatever views people might now hold with respect to the supposed militaristic character of early Islam, at least within the context of the period during which the Qur'an was being revealed, as Patricia Crone observes: "Justifying war appears to have been hard work" (2006: 456). As will become clear in what follows, while there are a substantial number of verses in the Qur'an that deal with the need to use violence in response to certain threats against the emerging Muslim community, the vast majority of these references are devoted either to outlining the various, often stringent, conditions under which armed conflict is permitted or to addressing the reluctance of the believers to engage in battle altogether.

At the same time, it cannot be denied that in the couple of centuries following the death of the Prophet, Islam and the Arabs experienced an unprecedented period of seemingly easy conquest and rapid expansion. This triumphant phase was facilitated by the disintegration of Byzantine, Persian and Roman power in the region, by the integration of

the Arab community, providing them with a collective potential well beyond what they were accustomed to when
they operated as single tribes or in loose confederacies, and
by the ideological support of Islam (Küng 2007: 168-70).
However, the fact that Islam was instrumental in helping
the Arabs to expand their military, political and commercial
power throughout the Middle East and beyond should not
be interpreted to suggest that the expansion of the religion
of Islam was the primary motivation for this activity. In fact,
the Arabs had a strict policy against forced conversion, as this
meant a loss in tax revenue from subjugated peoples and also
led to social and theological problems regarding the relative
status of Arab and non-Arab Muslims (Küng 2007: 174).

Just as it is important for us to question our understanding of the historical relationship between war and religious
conversion, we must be careful not to uncritically transpose
our current understanding, or more correctly our current
framing, of certain concepts and issues related to religious
conflict and violence back onto the Qur'an. The vocabulary
of war in the Qur'an centres around three concepts: *qital*, *harb* and jihad, and, as Abdel Haleem demonstrates, instructions relating to war cannot be understood outside the
overriding message of peace that the book contains (1999:
59-70). The concept of *qital*, which in most instances can
be unproblematically translated as killing, occurs 170 times
in the Qur'an, and, whether in the context of murder or
the slaying of an enemy in battle, is used primarily with reference to the individual act of taking another's life (Omar
2003: 443). By contrast, the word *harb* can be translated as
fighting, battle or war, and should be viewed as implying

collective opposition or a state of affairs related to conflict, without actually referring to a specific action; *harb* only occurs eleven times in the Qur'an (Omar 2003: 117).

The meaning of the word jihad, which appears forty-one times in the Qur'an, is most fundamentally associated with the idea of exertion or struggle, and even though it has now become synonymous with notions of holy war and terrorism, as Omar states: "Its meaning as war undertaken for the propagation of religion is unknown to the Arabic language and Islam" (2003: 106). As it is used in the Qur'an, the notion of jihad is unquestionably meant to imply a religious struggle, but the extent to which this can be equated to war rather than personal development remains a hotly debated topic and is discussed in more detail below. At the same time, however, consistent with the holistic view of Islam and the guidance provided in the Qur'an, the discussions that follow are predicated on the acceptance of the notion that there is no war that is not religious (Crone 2006: 456); as Hans Küng observes, from an Islamic perspective, war can never be holy (2007: 597).

IT NOW ALMOST sounds trite to observe that, since 9/11, the world has changed. Awareness of Islam has increased in Europe and North America, but it is less clear whether a corresponding increase in the understanding of Islam has taken place. The almost incomprehensible employment of commercial passenger aircraft as incendiary devices to destroy an iconic target and kill so many civilians has generated a global atmosphere of fear. The impact of the events in New York has been reinforced by similar but smaller scale attacks in England, Spain and Bali, to name a few, as well as by a growing tyranny of security, most palpable to anyone travelling by air. Notwithstanding these acts of aggression, however, the discourse of demonization that currently surrounds Muslims is largely informed by the academic and political response to Samuel Huntington's *Clash of Civilizations* (1998) and, to a lesser extent, Francis Fukuyama's *End of History* (1992), both of which were presaged by Arnold Toynbee's *Civilization on Trial* (1948).

In his capacity as a consultant for the Pentagon, Huntington developed a model of global dynamics through a process of carving up the nations of the world into a small set of supra-national complexes, one of which is conceived of as familiar and preferred, namely the West, and another, consisting of a somewhat arbitrary block of nations in which Islam is the predominant religion, is presented as foreign and dangerous. As Küng observes:

> In this way he provided ideological support, after the end of the Cold War, for the replacement of the hostile image of Communism with the hostile image of Islam, largely to justify a high level of American rearmament and, whether deliberately or not, to create a favourable atmosphere for further wars. (2007: xxiv)

Viewed from within this rhetorical framework, the events of 9/11 served to effectively shatter the myth of American invulnerability, while at the same time providing substance for the emerging myth of jihadist invincibility. Huntington's model was rapidly accepted as an explanation and a basis for value judgment regarding a range of events that included the growth of Islam as a religious and political force to be reckoned with internationally, the social challenges associated with the growth of Muslim populations in European countries, and the actual or merely the potential existence of unknown numbers of terrorist sleeper cells around the globe. No one spoke any longer of Islam, but rather of political Islam (Kepel 2002), radical Islam (Burke 2004), Islamic fundamentalism (Ali 2002) or, more succinctly, Islamism (Calvert 2008).

Mehdi Mozaffari defines Islamism as "a religious ideology with a holistic interpretation of Islam whose final aim is the conquest of the world by all means" (2007: 21). In discussing this four-part definition, the holistic view of Islam is seen to encompass the notions of religion (*din*), way of life (*dunya*) and government (*dawla*), a trinity of elements that describe a permanent and eternal state of existence (23). With respect to the concept of a religious ideology, because the cultural, religious, political and social realms of existence are inseparable within Islam, this expression is nearly tautological. However, Mozaffari points out that even though this way of thinking has its roots in the Qur'an:

> The Qur'an is not really a coherent book able to provide Muslims with clear and unambiguous guidelines. Roughly speaking, it is divided into two very different and somewhat contradictory sets of statements, principles and commandments. (21)

The first set corresponds to the period when the Prophet was still living in Makkah, with a religious attitude that was characterized by "relative moderation, toleration and pluralism," and the second set, which emerged following the migration to Madina, characterized by "politics, power and war." Mozaffari suggests that present divisions within the Islamic community are represented by cultural Muslims, who follow the early Makkan values, Islamists, who follow the Madinan values, and the vast majority of Muslims, who fall into a third category, drawing upon different Qur'anic precedents depending on the situation or circumstances. In an effort to move past some of this ambiguity, leaders such as Sayyid Qutb advocated a return to Islam in its original form—if the text of the Qur'an is to inform such an initiative, there is no way to determine what exactly that would mean (23).

Similarly, with the idea of the conquest of the world, this statement can be interpreted as the complete Islamicization of the globe, or it can mean the elimination of repression and imported values so that Islamic nations can live by their own standards. The means employed to achieve these ends span the range from "propagation, peaceful indoctrination and political struggle to violent methods such as assassination, hostage taking, terrorist and suicide actions, and even massacre of civil populations" (Mozaffari 2007: 24).

The remainder of this chapter is divided into four sections, the first two of which reflect the difference between individual and collective action, hence, killing and battle. The act of killing another human being does not necessarily occur solely within the context of war, so this section includes the subject of murder. I refer to the second section as "Battle" rather than "War" because, as Reuven Firestone points out, the majority of references to war in scripture and ancient historical accounts most often reflect single encounters between opposing parties, rather than the sort of sustained conflicts that would develop in later periods (1996: 101, n. 1). The section on jihad focuses on disentangling the related concepts of a personal spiritual challenge and the frame of mind required to take the life of another in defence of religion. Finally, I conclude with a discussion of terrorism, which as much as anything demonstrates the extent to which the meaning of the Qur'an can be shaped and recruited in support of particular ideologies.

※　※

Killing

As just stated, killing does not take place solely within the context of war. Similarly, not all killing is religiously motivated. Certainly, with respect to sanction and punishment, killing is a religious matter, but, as in contemporary legal proceedings, when trying to understand how killing is dealt with in the Qur'an, careful attention must be paid to the details of motive and opportunity. Sebastian Günther indicates that there are only two direct references to bloodshed in the Qur'an (2001: 240). The first of these (2:30) tells how the angels questioned God's decision to place humans on the Earth, arguing that people would cause damage and bloodshed, rather than offering praise. The second (2:84) refers to the promise extracted from the Israelites not to shed each other's blood or drive one another from their homelands. While stopping short of identifying the propensity to kill others as an inherent characteristic of humans, these verses at least appear to suggest that shedding the blood of another human being is contrary to the will of God.

Mohammad Fadel explains that killing is viewed as murder in the Qur'an when it refers to infanticide (6:140) or the intentional killing of another without just cause (5:32), such as punishment for murder or highway robbery (2003: 458). While the punishment for infanticide is said to come in the afterlife, in the latter instance, the Qur'an advocates seeking an alternate remedy, such as financial compensation (2:178, 17:33) rather taking a life for a life. On the basis of 4:93, it would appear that murder is the only crime other than associating others with God that merits eternal damnation (459).

The first mention of killing in the fourth surah (4:29-30) is preceded by a discussion of how a man who cannot afford to marry a free believing woman should marry a believing slave instead (4:25-28). The verses are followed by the admonition not to covet what others have (4:31-33). Thus, from the co-text, it is reasonable to suggest that the reference to killing in these verses should be understood within the context of fair dealing in trade or economic wellbeing.

> You who believe, do not wrongfully consume each
> other's wealth but trade by mutual consent. Do not kill
> each other, for God is merciful to you. If any of you does
> these things out of hostility and injustice, We shall make
> him suffer Fire: that is easy for God. (4:29-30)

This passage appears to acknowledge that some individuals have killed others either for stealing their goods or for having cheated them in a business deal. Honesty and justice are being advocated and killing is clearly forbidden on punishment of eternal damnation.

In some cases this particular injunction against killing has been translated as, "Nor kill (or destroy) yourselves" (Yusuf Ali), which, as will discussed below in the section on terrorism, has been taken to mean that Muslims are not to commit suicide. In isolation, this statement may be open to this alternate interpretation, but when the passage is viewed in its entirety there is little justification for treating it in this manner.

The most extensive coverage of the subject of killing is found in a long passage (4:88-94), situated roughly in the middle of the Battle Block (4:71-104). This passage appears to be divided into two distinct sequences of nearly equal length, the first of which (4:88-91) deals with the hypocrites; the second (4:92-94) addresses the situation of one believer killing another believer.

The unstated premise for the first sequence appears to be that certain Muslims were unsure how to respond to the hypocrites. The initial verse (88) questions this uncertainty, indicating that only God can bring people to faith and that those He has left to go astray cannot be brought back through human effort. The second verse (89) indicates that the hypocrites would like to turn the faithful away from God and therefore the Muslims are not to accept them as allies or supporters until they migrate to Madina and join with the Muslims, both in faith and in defence of the community. The final statement of the verse indicates that if the hypocrites turn on the faithful, then they are to be seized and killed. The next verse (90) indicates, however, that if the hypocrites seek refuge with a neutral party, withdraw from fighting or offer peace, then the Muslims are to take no action against them. The last verse (91) in this sequence addresses those who we might view as the truly hypocritical among the hypocrites—those who back down from confrontation when they are in danger, but who once again advocate aggression when they are safe. God gives the Muslims clear authority to deal with these people by seizing and killing them.

The second sequence opens with an unambiguous statement (92) that a Muslim should never kill another Muslim except by mistake. The circumstances of such an occurrence are not spelled out, but one can imagine what is now referred to as a friendly fire accident, or we might imagine that an individual who had been an opponent of Islam (or perhaps one who had lapsed from the faith after initially believing) had now accepted Islam, but some other individual was not aware of this at the time they confronted and killed them. The remainder of this initial verse provides specifics as to the appropriate level of compensation to be paid, depending upon the social position of the slain individual and the heir's relationship to the deceased. Unlike the conditions that merit capital punishment (5:32), the Qur'an does not condone taking a life for a life in this instance. The middle verse (93) in this sequence succinctly states that if a Muslim deliberately takes the life of another Muslim, then the punishment for him is Hell. The final verse (94) is a precautionary note, warning Muslims not to act on the assumption that someone is not a Muslim, in order to acquire some gain in this life. The verse is quite specific in saying that if someone offers you a greeting of peace you are not to say to them that they are not a believer. Only God knows the truth and it is better to err on the side of caution.

When these two sequences are examined together, it is fair to suggest that the Qur'an does not advocate killing, and that in those instances when killing is permitted, there is little or no ambiguity surrounding the circumstances under which such an action can take place.

�֎   ✖

Battle

As Crone points out, in the Qur'an, fighting is deemed as legitimate if it is done in self-defence, in response to aggression or to punish wrongdoing (2006: 456). For the most part, when the need arises, Muslims are encouraged to fight (e.g., 2:244, 4:71, 8:65), but they are rarely ordered to do so (457). Several verses would appear to suggest that the Muslims had little taste for war, with many of them arguing that they did not want to fight their kinsmen (9:49), or that they could not leave their homes (33:13) or their flocks and families (48:11). As a result, turnout was normally insufficient to ensure victory or minimize losses (4:75, 9:38), and those who stayed home were deemed to be sick of heart (9:81), afraid of death (47:20) or closer to unbelief than to faith (3:167).

Anyone familiar with the Torah will recall that much of the text is consumed with recounting the wanderings of the Israelites in the period between their deliverance from Egypt and their entry into the Promised Land. In the Qur'an, one passage (5:22-29) relates the story of the spies from the book of Numbers (13:1-14:45), in which the Israelites are condemned to sojourn in the wilderness for forty years as punishment for their refusal to fight. This story is particularly germane to the overall message of the Qur'an because, as already stated, the Muslims demonstrated continued reluctance to fight in defence of God's cause—the establishment of the Islamic community. Another significant story of battle, in this case from the first book of Samuel (17), is that of David and Goliath (2:247-251), in which a physically weaker force is able to overcome a much stronger foe with the help of God. The message for the emerging Islamic community again seems clear.

Rizwi Faizer describes four events that took place prior to or during the life of Muhammad that are mentioned in the Qur'an (17:4-8, 30:1-5, 85:4-9, 105:1-5) and which appear to match historical incidents (2002: 146-48). The first of these is the destruction of Jerusalem, with the verses being interpreted to indicate either two or three occurrences, and various commentators suggesting that these were the ones that took place at the hands of Sennacherib (701 BCE), Nebuchadnezzar (587 BCE), Antiochus (167 BCE) or Titus (70 CE). The second event took place during the lifetime of the Prophet and is seen to refer to the ongoing conflicts between the Byzantines, Persians and Romans to the north of the Arabian peninsula (613-624 CE). Both of these passages would be interpreted as presaging the eventual conquest by Islamic forces of Jerusalem (and hence Judaism) and what was left of the Roman provinces in the east (and hence Christianity and paganism).

The third and fourth incidents appear to apply more directly to the Muslims, with the first of these often interpreted as reflecting the mistreatment of Muslims by members of the Quraysh tribe. However, the passage is alternately understood to recount the story of a Jewish king of Yemen who burned a group of Christians when they refused to convert to Judaism. The final event is often interpreted to have taken place in the year of Muhammad's birth (570), and it tells how God employed an army of birds to turn away forces from Abyssinia that were employing elephants to attack Makkah and potentially destroy the Ka'ba.

Several verses have been linked to battles that took place during the period of revelation, each of which presents a particular change in the rules of engagement followed by the Muslims (Faizer 2002: 149-51). One verse (2:217) justifies fighting during the sacred months, and it is associated with the expedition to Nakhla (623 CE), in which the Prophet did not participate. Another verse (8:41), associated with the battle of Badr (624), establishes that one fifth of the booty from war is to be set aside for the Prophet and for distribution to the needy. Another verse (16:127), which forbids the mutilation of bodies after combat, is linked to the battle of Uhud (625), in which the Prophet was wounded, and after which the body of the Prophet's uncle Hamza was mutilated by the enemy. Finally, after the raid on the Banu l-Nadir (625), one verse (59:6) states that property taken without force belongs to the Prophet. It is important to keep in mind that the precise interpretation of these verses and the establishment of their linkage to specific historical events is purely inferential, based on tradition, and cannot be determined solely from the text of the Qur'an.

Faizer indicates that exegetes through the ages have generally agreed that the clearest statement of victory in the

Qur'an does not occur with respect to a battle but with respect to the establishment of the Treaty of Hudaybiyya (2002: 149). The key verse related to this treaty is: "Truly We have opened up a path to clear triumph for you [Prophet]" (48:1). Tariq Ramadan explains that the treaty had four essential points: the right of the Prophet and his companions to visit the holy sites in Makkah in the following year, a ten-year truce between the people of Makkah and Madina, the extension of the terms of the agreement to cover any tribe or clan that allied themselves with either side, and special conditions pertaining to asylum seekers from either city (2007: 155). When a tribe allied to the Makkans broke the truce by attacking another tribe, the Prophet prepared his forces for battle and headed towards Makkah. According to tradition, when he arrived, he prayed in the sanctuary, destroyed the idols in the Ka'ba and publicly recited a number of key verses from the Qur'an, but he did not permit his forces to engage in any fighting with the people of the city. As Ramadan eloquently states:

> The Prophet had come back to the place of origin of his mission. He had experienced persecution, then exile, then war, and he was returning to the source in peace, with the aura of victory. More than the physical path of a life, this was the initiatory journey of a heart and conscience going through the stages of the great jihad that takes people from the natural tension of passions to the peace of spiritual education. (2007: 179)

The subject of jihad is dealt with in the next section, but the following analysis serves to bring together the understanding of the physical and spiritual components that constitute the notion of holy war. Reuven Firestone, in his comparative analysis of the roots of holy war in Jewish and Islamic scripture, points out that the expression "holy war" was coined by the German scripture scholar Friedrich Schwally, mentioned earlier as playing a major role in establishing the chronological ordering of the surahs, in a book by that name (*Heilige Krieg / Holy War*) in 1901 (Firestone 1996: 101). The concept of holy war is at least implicit in the scripture of the Jews, with several passages in Deuteronomy advocating war as a means of acquiring the Promised Land (e.g., 1:6-8, 3:1-22, 11:23-25) and as a way of ridding the land of idolatry and idolaters (e.g., 7:1-5, 12:1-3, 18:9-14). Firestone points out that the dictates regarding the eradication of idolatry were restricted to actions carried out within the sacred land and were not to be interpreted as a universal sanction (1996: 105). Within these limits, the existence of idolatry was viewed as worse than killing.

With respect to support for holy war in the Qur'an, Firestone suggests that the Islamic understanding of these matters was established as early as the 8th century and has been passed on, without substantial critical reflection, to contemporary scholars in the West (1996: 110). The notion is seen to have gone through four stages of development, reflecting the progressive revelation of the Qur'an over a twenty year period, the particular circumstances of revelation, and the assumption that those verses which were revealed towards the end of the Prophet's life abrogated some or all of the earlier verses that dealt with the same subject matter. In the early stages in Makkah, when the primary objective was to establish an initial group of followers (15:94-95), fighting was not permitted. In the second stage following the migration to Madina (22:39-40), believers were given permission to fight in defence of their community. The third stage was characterized by the initiation of offensive action in the form of caravan raids against Makkan traders (2:191). Finally, according to this scheme, Muslims were enjoined to attack their opponents at all times and in all places. In the Qur'an, the largest clusters of war related verses are found in surahs 2, 8 and 9 (2:190-217, 8:15-19, 8:38-45, 8:59-66, 9:1-33, 9:119-123), and the three key verses associated with this final stage of development are 2:216, 9:5 and 9:29.

Putting aside, for the moment, a detailed examination of the specific content of these three verses, and continuing with Firestone's argument, he suggests that as the Islamic community became a more coherent and organized social and political entity, its existential anxiety over the continued refusal by the members of some groups to adhere to its religious values and expectations increased.

> As it grew in strength, therefore, the Muslim community ironically came to regard the continued existence of polytheism and non-Muslim expressions of monotheism as a growing threat—at this stage, not so much to its physical survival as a threat to its prestige and self-concept as the religion of truth. (1996: 113)

As a result, unlike the military actions sanctioned in Deuteronomy and played out the books of Joshua and Judges, the Muslims made a peaceful entry into Makkah. Thus they were able to neutralize their major source of opposition by showing mercy and avoiding bloodshed, which gains special significance from the fact that much of the fighting would have been between kinsmen. Despite the fact that victory was achieved in this instance through peaceful means, and despite the fact that Firestone describes the physical threat to Islam as secondary, he goes on to suggest that the Qur'an advocates continued militancy, as evidenced by the following verse.

> So [believers] do not lose heart and cry out for peace. It is you who have the upper hand: God is with you. He will not begrudge you the reward for your [good] deeds. (47:35)

No rationale is offered for the selection of this particular verse in support of his contention, nor is any analysis of the content and context of the verse provided. A brief examination of this verse and the surah in which it is found, however, suggests some intriguing possibilities.

Surah 47 (*Muhammad*) is a relatively short surah (38 verses) from the Madinan period and there is no question that it deals almost exclusively with the subject of war. Among other things, it addresses the reluctance of the Muslim people to continue their struggle against hypocrites, apostates and those who go out of their way to prevent the faithful from practising their religion. One verse stands out for comment:

> We have destroyed many a town stronger than your own [Prophet]—the town which [chose to] expel you—and they had no one to help them. (47:13)

There can be little doubt that the city being referred to is Makkah. When this verse is read in conjunction with the verse cited by Firestone, it would appear as if the Qur'an is warning the Muslims that they should not be lured into complacency by what took place in the holy city and that while God acknowledges their efforts to this point, there is still (military) work to be done to ensure victory for Islam—albeit with God's help.

The fact that surah 47 is referred to as *Muhammad* provides another possible clue to Firestone's interpretation. At the simplest level, this designation can be understood as a reflection of the fact that the Prophet is mentioned by name in the second verse. At a more complex level, given the subject matter of the surah, it is conceivable that some commentators might interpret this designation as a deliberate association of Muhammad with the act of waging war. One of the critical facts to bear in mind, though, is that the naming of the surahs is a product of Muslim scholarship long after the period of revelation.

Returning to the comparison set up by Firestone, he also suggests that the limitation set out in Deuteronomy with respect to the eradication of idolatry is altered in the Qur'an. That is, he identifies several verses as providing outright justification for unrestricted violence against idolatry and idolaters, raising the status of war to a holy act (e.g., 3:157-158, 4:74-76, 9:20-22, 47:4-8). He cites one verse in particular as providing a succinct and explicit statement of this mission.

> So fight them until there is no more idolatry, and religion is entirely God's. (8:39)

If we accept the translation of this verse as presented by Firestone then we might be open to his interpretation, but turning to several other translations (Yusuf Ali, Pickthall,

Arberry and Abdel Haleem) we find that he is alone in using the word idolatry in this case. The others all understand the first part of the verse to be referring to persecution, for example, as in Abdel Haleem's translation:

> [Believers], fight them until there is no more persecution, and all worship is devoted to God alone. (8:39)

Irrespective of the fact that Firestone appears to be overstating the contrast between the Jewish and Islamic conceptions of holy war, it is quite clear from the verses we have examined thus far that even though war is justified and carried out by Muslims in response to persecution, it is done so with great reluctance.

OF THE THREE verses that are commonly cited in support of war (2:216, 9:5, 9:29), I refer to the first of these as the Carte Blanche Verse, because it appears to declare open season with respect to engaging in violence, to the extent that it identifies no specific target and no limiting conditions, and because it provides an unparalleled example of how the text and interpretation of the Qur'an can be shaped to reflect certain religious and political interests.

> Fighting is ordained for you, though you dislike it. You may dislike something although it is good for you, or like something although it is bad for you: God knows and you do not. (2:216)

Taken on its own, the first part of this verse would appear to establish fighting as a religious obligation—an integral component of the everyday life of all Muslims, while at the same time recognizing that this might be contrary to the will and sentiment of the people. It is also important to point out that the Arabic word being translated as fighting in this instance is the word *qital*. This is an important point because in the so-called King Fahd translation of the Qur'an the opening phrase of this verse is presented as: "Jihad is ordained for you." This translation, prepared by Muhammad Hilali and Muhammad Khan (1997), is printed and distributed by the King Fahd Complex in Madina, Saudi Arabia, and is officially recognized by Saudi religious scholars as authoritative—it is the translation that is distributed to pilgrims during *hajj*. At the risk of digressing into a polemical diatribe, the irony of this, what might be called reverse translation and strategic substitution of terms merits at least one comment. Surely it is outside the purview of any interpreter/translator to rewrite the Qur'an.

Putting politics aside and returning to the analysis of the verse, the surrounding text provides critical information with respect to how this verse should be interpreted. While any segmentation of passages from the Qur'an can be viewed as arbitrary, and performed in the service of the interpreter, an appropriate understanding of the verse in question is more likely to emerge when it is read as part of an extended passage (2:189-218) that itself is part of a much longer sequence of verses that contain instructions regarding the religious obligations of the emerging Muslim community. The predominant theme of the extended passage is the performance of the pilgrimage to Makkah (*hajj*, discussed in the next chapter), with the subject of the pilgrimage being introduced briefly in verse 189 and the long sequence from verse 196 to verse 215 providing details of the ritual and describing the relationship between the performance of appropriate actions in this life and the attainment of reward in the hereafter. This leaves two sequences (2:190-195 and 2:216-218) that deal with fighting.

Examining these sequences in reverse order, of the two verses that follow the oft-cited verse 216 the shorter second verse (218) clearly marks a punctuation point in the text, as it constitutes a sort of promissory note for those who believe and strive in God's cause, and it ends with a pair of divine names (most forgiving and merciful). The significantly longer verse (217) provides a direct link back to verse 189, in that it discusses the appointed time (sacred month) for the performance of the pilgrimage. It also returns to issues raised in the initial fighting sequence (2:190-195) by addressing the concern among the believers about fighting in the sacred month, saying that it is a greater offense for some to bar the faithful from performing their religious duties than it is to take up arms against these opponents—"persecution is worse than killing."

The initial fighting sequence (2:190-195) is composed primarily of short imperative sentences that instruct the believers to fight and kill those who would fight against them in the sacred place. Verse 192 is especially informative in that its states: "but if they stop, then God is most forgiving and merciful." The use of the divine names provides a clear signal that this sequence is to be read in conjunction with the corresponding sequence (2:216-218) at the close of this longer passage. The sequence goes on to state that any action taken against opponents must be a proportional response and that Muslims are never to initiate hostilities. As a final note on this sequence, Abdel Haleem points out that over the span of six relatively short verses there are four outright prohibitions and six restrictions against fighting (1999: 64).

Taking into account the co-text of the Carte Blanche Verse, it is difficult to understand how this verse has come to provide any justification for holy war. Rather than establishing divine sanction for open hostility and aggression, this verse unambiguously grants permission for Muslims to take up arms against anyone who would prevent them from performing the pilgrimage, during the appointed time and within the sacred space. More restrictively, it is reasonable to suggest that the permission granted in this verse only made sense up until the Muslims gained control of Makkah in 630.

With respect to anti-Islamic rhetoric about the inseparability of the religion of Islam from the notion of holy war, mention of the Sword Verse (9:5) is about as common as mention of the phrase "Islam was spread by the sword," but, ironically, the verse does not even contain the word sword.

> When the [four] forbidden months are over, wherever you encounter the idolaters, kill them, seize them, besiege them, wait for them at every lookout post; but if they turn [to God], maintain the prayer, and pay the prescribed alms, let them go on their way, for God is most forgiving and merciful. (9:5)

In contrast to the verse just examined (2:216), this verse contains multiple instructions and conditions. It begins with a temporal condition, indicating that for fully one-third of the year Muslims are not to engage in acts of aggression. A specific target group (idolaters) is identified and, while the instructions to seize and kill members of this group parallel the content of related verses, the instructions to besiege and ambush idolaters, unique to this verse, sound more like collective action on one hand and surreptitious or premeditated action on the other. The verse also includes an escape clause for the idolaters, but it requires that these individuals not only recognize God, but that they live according to the prescribed practices of Islam by praying regularly and paying alms. Finally, the use of the divine names (most forgiving and merciful) suggests that this verse should be considered in concert with the two sequences on fighting that we have already examined (2:19-195 and 2:216-218).

Looking at the placement of this verse within the surah, it is part of a much longer passage (9:1-15) that discusses the frustrations of dealing with those who, even though they have concluded a peace treaty with the Muslims—one that establishes rights of religious practice and access to holy sites—persist in breaking the terms of the agreement. The sense of rage and frustration is palpable in the text, and as Abdel Haleem points out, the target of this instruction to fight is a group of "hardened polytheists in Arabia, who would accept nothing other than the expulsion of the Muslims or their reversion to paganism" (1999: 65).

The verse (9:6) immediately following the Sword Verse says that if any one of the idolaters seeks the Prophet's protection, then that individual is to be sheltered in a safe place and given the opportunity to hear the word of God. The very next verse (9:7) indicates that even though it might sound counterintuitive for Muslims to establish and honor a treaty with idolaters (people who clearly do not accept the truth about God), provided they abide by the conditions of the treaty then they are to be left alone.

As in the case of the Carte Blanche Verse, it is difficult to determine how the Sword Verse ever came to be understood as granting blanket permission for Muslims to wage war against non-Muslims. I have not been able to find any adequate discussion of how this verse got its name.

The last of the three key verses to be examined in this section is the Tribute Verse.

> Fight those of the People of the Book who do not [truly] believe in God and the Last Day, who do not forbid what God and His Messenger have forbidden, who do not obey the rule of justice, until they pay the tax and agree to submit. (9:29)

In contrast to the previous verse (9:5), which refers to idolaters, this verse is directed at the People of the Book, but its message is somewhat ambiguous. The Muslims are to fight a certain subset of the People of the Book who do not comply with four religious conditions, one of which is associated with Muhammad. Arguably, the only group of people that could possibly fulfill this set of conditions would be Muslims and yet this verse appears to allow for some individuals who recognize the truth of Islam but who have not themselves become Muslims. A fifth condition specifies adherence to justice and given the proximity of this verse to the passage discussed above (9:1-15) it is reasonable to assume that what is being referred to is a treaty or some other form of agreement that allows this group to peacefully co-exist with Muslims. The validity of this assumption is reinforced by a direct reference to the Sacred Mosque in the verse (9:28) preceding the Tribute Verse. The sixth condition seems to specify that part of the agreement involves the payment of a tax; if this tax is paid, then members of this group will be left alone. The final condition to submit introduces some added complexity. If this condition simply implies submission to justice and therefore payment of the appropriate tax, then this latter part of the verse is quite clear. However, when this final condition is read along with verses that follow the Tribute Verse, other possibilities for interpretation emerge.

Verses 30 through 35 delineate the mistakes in belief that have been made by the Jews and Christians, for example the Christian claim that Jesus is the son of God, and they point out the misdeeds of rabbis and priests. The content of these verses would appear to suggest that the requirement to submit at the end of verse 29 should be interpreted to mean that people will submit to Islam, in which case the instruction to fight could be interpreted to imply forced conversion rather than killing. While the resolution of this interpretive matter remains open, whatever the case might be, an examination of this verse exposes yet another instance where it is difficult to determine how any interpretation that claims to be consistent with the overall message of the Qur'an could be seen to justify waging of holy war.

The Sword Verse and the Tribute Verse are contained in surah 9 (*Repentance/al-Tawbah*), and it is worth noting that this is the only surah in the Qur'an that does not begin with the *basmalah* (In the name of God, the Lord of Mercy, the Giver of Mercy). There are two frequently cited explanations for this omission. First, Yusuf Ali explains that the Prophet had instructed that this surah was to follow surah 8 (*Battle Gains/al-Anfal*), but his instructions left the scribes uncertain about whether it was meant to be a separate surah, and so the *basmalah* was left out (2004: 435). Second, given that the initial verses of the surah contain instructions to kill, commentators speculated that the juxtaposition of these instructions with an invocation of divine mercy would only serve to confuse the intention of the message (Gwynne 2006: 66).

Shifting to contemporary global concerns and taking into account the preceding discussions, the following observation by Abdel Haleem provides an appropriate note on which to close out this section:

> In the sphere of war and peace, there is nothing in the Qur'an or hadith which should cause Muslims to feel unable to sign and act according to modern international conventions, and there is much in the Qur'an and hadith from which modern international law can benefit. (1999: 69)

❋   ❋

Jihad

The brief discussion on the subject of jihad that follows could have been included in any one of the other sections in this chapter, but I wanted to avoid the sort of reductionist approach to the matter that is prevalent in much contemporary literature about the relationship between violence and Islam.

As evidenced by the rendering of the Carte Blanche Verse (2:216) in the King Fahd translation of the Qur'an, which I discussed in the previous section, there appears to be a systemic taken-for-grantedness in the global rhetoric about jihad, whether emerging from inside or outside Islam, that for the most part now serves to prevent us from even questioning the assumed equivalence of jihad and violence, let alone allowing for a systematic effort to gain a more fulsome understanding of what the Qur'an has to say on the matter. There are two primary points to be made.

First, even though it is clear that the Qur'an grants permission for the Muslims to fight and to kill, these acts of violence were only to take place under very strict conditions of time, place and target, and only for defensive purposes against outright attacks or persecution. As Tariq Ramadan expresses it: "The essence of *jihad* is the quest for peace, and *qital* is, at times, the necessary path to peace" (2007: 99).

Second, if the principle meaning of the concept of jihad in the Qur'an is not associated with violence, then how exactly are we to understand it?

[S]o do not give in to the disbelievers: strive hard against them with this Qur'an. (25:52)

Ramadan indicates that this is the first use of the term jihad in the Qur'an and that it carries the double meaning of making an effort and of resisting oppression and persecution (2007: 52). Furthermore, this verse could not be any clearer with respect to how these actions are to be carried out—the weapon of jihad is the Qur'an. In the fourth surah, this question is asked about the hypocrites: "Will they not think about this Qur'an?" (4:82). A few verses further on we read: "We have sent down the Scripture to you [Prophet] so that you can judge between people in accordance with what God has shown you" (4:105). Not only is the Qur'an the weapon of jihad it is the principle mechanism through which to avoid conflict and make the proper determination with respect to when action is required. In the early period of Islam it is also clear that this weapon was to be used against the self as much as it was to be used against others, as explained in the hadith literature.

According to al-Bayhaqi, following the military expedition to Hunayn in 630, the Prophet announced to his troops that they were returning from the lesser jihad to the greater jihad—that of fighting the self. Ramadan eloquently, and perhaps rather idealistically, describes the distinction as follows:

> For the Muslims, as for all human beings, this inner struggle was the most difficult, the most noble, and the one that required the most understanding, forgiveness, and, of course, sincerity to oneself. War and its lesser *jihad* had shown how difficult it was to die for God; daily life and its greater *jihad* now showed Muslims that it is even more difficult to live for God, in light, transparence, coherence, spiritual demand, patience, and peace. (Ramadan 2007: 194)

So, it appears that the concept of jihad has more to do with personal struggle than it does with violence directed toward others, and at least according to the hadith literature the personal struggle of faith is by far the more important and difficult of the two. What remains to be explored before moving on to a discussion of terrorism are the questions of what else the Qur'an has to say about the concept and of how we arrived at our present understanding of it.

Ella Landau-Tasseron explains that of the forty-one occurrences of the word jihad in the Qur'an, five of them are related to swearing oaths, and of the remaining thirty-six, on the basis of linguistic and thematic analysis, only ten can be said to relate directly to war (2003: 36). Evidence for this association comes from the military content and context of the verses in which the word is found (e.g., 4:95, 5:54, 9:41), with all of these references linked specifically to the emigrants—those who travelled from Makkah to Madina with the Prophet in 622. In trying to interpret the more frequent uses of the term, commentators have suggested such meanings as struggling against one's own desires and weaknesses, persevering in the observance of religious law, seeking religious knowledge, observing the sunnah, obeying God and summoning people to worship (37). Landau-Tasseron points out in this regard that one of the most paradigmatic uses of the word is in the verse: "Strive hard for God as is His due" (22:78), part of a longer passage in which Muslims are instructed to "perform the religious duties originally prescribed to Abraham" (38).

Mark Juergensmeyer explains that our contemporary association of the concept of jihad with violence owes much to the writings of Muhammad Abd al-Salam Faraj, who argued that the Qur'an and hadith were primarily about warfare and that Muslims over the centuries had neglected their duty in this regard by relying on peaceful and legal means to deal with apostasy and other challenges to Islam (2003: 82). Among other things, Faraj advocated the use of deceit and trickery to fight the infidel, for which the true Muslim soldier would be rewarded with a place in Paradise. He was executed in 1982 for his part in the assassination of Anwar Sadat. Faraj certainly had predecessors, of whom the two most important were Maulana Abu al-Ala Mawdudi in Pakistan and Sayyid Qutb in Egypt, an influential member of the Muslim Brotherhood, who was imprisoned for his ideas in the early 1950s, finally being executed in 1966. Juergensmeyer notes that the ideas of Mawdudi, Qutb and Faraj continue to flourish as they are circulated widely through Muslim clergy and through the Islamic educational system (84). Evidence for this assessment can be found in the very existence of the Taliban (the Arabic word for student).

Terrorism

The idea of terrorism, while certainly not new, has taken on startling new dimensions over the past few decades, not all of which are linked to the religion of Islam or to the ideologies and actions of individual Muslims. However, as Bruce Hoffman remarks with respect to the events of September 11, 2001:

> on that day long-standing suppositions that terrorists were more interested in publicity than in killing and that terrorists who justified violence with theological imperatives were no more bloody-minded than their secular counterparts were swept aside in a deafening crescendo of death and destruction. (2006: ix)

In broad terms, the roots of terrorism have been associated with responses to decadence, repression, oppression, desecration and a host of other atrocities, real or perceived. With particular reference to Islam, rationalizations for terrorist actions have been couched in rhetoric about efforts to impose democratic forms of government, about the corrupting effects of free market capitalism and about pointed attacks on religious values, as in the cases of the publication of Salman Rushdie's *Satanic Verses* or the Danish newspaper cartoons of Muhammad (Gregersen 2009). Whatever its origins or consequences, terrorism, most often linked in some way to Islam, influences daily events around the world. The issues examined in this section include the relationship between fear and terrorism, the use of the Qur'an to justify terrorism and the related matters of suicide, martyrdom and reward.

The notion of fear as it pertains to terror and terrorism is distinct from a related idea that is critical to understanding the message of the Qur'an, and which is often expressed as the fear of God (*taqwa*, discussed in the next chapter). As Scott Alexander explains, there are several words in the Qur'an that imply some aspect of fear and which are usually translated using such words as fright, caution, trembling, quaking and shuddering (2002: 197-98). Some verses (3:151, 8:12, 33:26, 59:2) refer to the fact that God will strike terror into the hearts of the unbelievers or those who oppress the faithful. What is clear from the majority of these references, however, is that they represent an eschatological notion of what people will face in the life to come, should they fail to heed God's word. Few, if any, can be interpreted to reflect the idea of fear for life and limb.

There is one verse that might be viewed as reflecting our contemporary notions of terrorism and violent attacks:

> I shall put terror into the hearts of the disbelievers—strike above their necks and strike all their finger tips" (8:12).

In keeping with the trend among exegetes to interpret this verse militaristically, Yusuf Ali suggests that the imagery invoked here is consistent with what could happen if one attacked an armed man—he might be afraid, but while his armor would protect his heart, cutting off his head would finish him or cutting off his hands would at least render him unable to continue fighting (2004: 417). Beyond sounding like sage tactical advice for combatants, Yusuf Ali's explanation takes some of the apocalyptic sting out of a verse that might come across upon first reading.

Ingrid Mattson states that, beginning with the act of Mu'awiyya's soldiers placing pages of the Qur'an on their lances both to signal the righteousness of their position and as a means of avoiding attack at Siffin in 657, "there have been Muslims who have used the Qur'an to encourage, justify, and challenge highly specific political agendas, some violent and intolerant" (2008: 183).

Perhaps no name is more synonymous with Islamic terrorism than that of Osama bin Laden. Bruce Lawrence explains that bin Laden is waging a double war against infidels both outside and inside Islam, identified respectively as the "Zionist-Crusaders" and the ruling families of Saudi Arabia, who are condemned for their collusion with the West and their desecration of the holy sites of Islam (2006: 173). Bin

Laden claims to take his inspiration from the Qur'an, but as Lawrence indicates:

> For him the Qur'an is a book with only one Sign: kill the infidel in the name of Allah, pursue jihad as defensive holy war, no matter the cost or the carnage. (2006: 172)

The specific passages to which bin Laden refers at the beginning of his 1996 *Declaration of War* (3:102, 4:1, 33:70-71) speak primarily of one's duty to God, but following the commentaries of the jurist Ibn Taymiyya (d. 1328) and the exegete al-Qurtubi (d. 1273), this duty is interpreted to mean the waging of defensive war (jihad) against Islam's enemies. As suggested above, the range of enemies is quite extensive and for bin Laden any war that Muslims might engage in is defensive because Islam's very existence is perpetually under attack from inside and out.

As part of his call to arms, bin Laden positions himself as a modern day Shuayb (prophet to the people of Midian), who in seeking social justice used his own wealth to support his initiatives, calling upon others to do the same, as described in this passage from the Qur'an:

> He answered, "My people can you not see? What if I am acting on clear evidence from my Lord? He Himself has given me good provision: I do not want to do what I am forbidding you to do, I only want to put things right as far as I can. I cannot succeed without God's help: I trust in Him, and always turn to Him. (11:88)

In setting out to "put things right," bin Laden uses the initial portion of the Sword Verse as his primary proof text, but he does so by completely ignoring the limiting instruc-

tions contained in the second part of the verse and by failing to develop a broader understanding of the verse in light
of the material contained in the verses that precede and
follow it. Lawrence's frustration with his subject is palpable
and he does not mince words when it comes to assessing
bin Laden's mission and method.

> What is the end of Osama bin Laden's project? It is nei-
> ther an Islamic state nor a restoration of the Caliphate. In-
> stead it promotes nothing but endless anarchy. Osama bin
> Laden has been mislabelled as an Islamic fundamentalist.
> He is more the descendant of Rasputin and the Russian
> anarchists of the early 20th century than he is of Muham-
> mad and Muslim warriors of the early 7th century. His
> Qur'an is not a signpost but a grave marker. (2006: 183)

Lawrence is not alone in taking such a strong position.
In her systematic and thorough analysis of bin Laden's writings, Rosalind Gwynne concludes that "he makes not even
a pretence of hoping for peaceful resolution of the issues in
that he does not, in his own voice, clearly invite the enemy
to accept Islam" (2006: 88). Gwynne goes on to explain
that bin Laden's reasoning is grounded in three techniques:
first, he follows Ibn Taymiyya and Abd al-Salam Faraj in
claiming that "jihad in Islam is more important than anything else except belief in God;" second, he takes verses
from the Qur'an out of context, especially the Sword Verse;
and third, he alters or distorts the meaning of words, particularly with regards to who counts as an apostate (88).

Bin Laden is not alone in offering contemporary interpretations of the Qur'an in support of terrorism. Joas
Wagemakers describes the way in which Jordanian Abu

Muhammad al-Maqdisi interprets the notion of enemies in surah 60 (*Women Tested/al-Mumtahana*) to inform an agenda aimed at overthrowing the political rulers of the Muslim world (2008: 352). According to one American research report, al-Maqdisi is considered to be "the key contemporary ideologue in the jihadi intellectual universe" and "the most influential living jihadi theorist" (qtd. in Wagemakers 2008: 349). As was the case with bin Laden, it is instructive to recognize that their efforts are directed internally as much if not more than they are directed outside of Islam.

There can be little doubt that the hadith literature forbids Muslims from committing suicide, as seen in the following example:

> And do not kill yourself, for God is merciful to you.
> Whoever kills himself with an iron weapon, then the iron weapon will remain in his hand and he will continually stab himself in the belly with it in the fire of hell eternally, for ever and ever; whoever kills himself by drinking poison will eternally drink poison in hellfire, and whoever kills himself by falling off a mountain will fall for ever in the fire of hell. (qtd. in Ali and Post 2008: 626)

I have two reasons for citing this particular hadith. First, the level of detail it contains clearly demonstrates the perception of the severity of the crime of taking one's life. Second, all of the examples given reflect the action of an individual taking their life/death into their own hands, in a sense usurping the prerogative of God. The outstanding question in the present context, then, is whether taking one's life for God can be assessed as theologically different from the acts mentioned in this hadith.

Many scholars suggest that suicide is forbidden in the Qur'an (specifically in 2:195 and 4:29), but in contrast to the numerous explicit prohibitions that can be found in the hadith literature there is no clear evidence to support this understanding (Hoffman 2006: 159). At best, the central phrase in the first of these verses: "do not contribute to your destruction with your own hands" (2:195) can be understood as a general injunction against doing anything that you know will cause you harm (Abdel Haleem 2005: 22). In light of these remarks, it is difficult to imagine what foundation can be found in Islam to justify the suicide bombings that have become a fundamental component of the tactics of terrorism.

Farhana Ali and Jerrold Post suggest that the origin of committing suicide in the service of jihad can be found in the writings of Shia theologian Ayatollah Sayyid Muhammad Husayn Fadlallah, who, as a means of avoiding ongoing debates about the whether or not suicide was prohibited in Islam, argued that to die as a suicide bomber is the same as soldiers entering a battle in which they know they will die (2008: 624). Theologically, Fadlallah's argument shifts the assessment of the act of suicide from one of murder to one of martyrdom. No matter how flimsy the logic might be, the practical effect of the rhetoric has been powerful, with one terror scholar reporting that between March 2003 and February 2006, there were 443 suicide attacks in Iraq (633).

As with the subject of suicide, the Qur'an does not say anything directly about martyrs—those who are killed for their faith. As Wim Raven explains, the Islamic concept of martyrdom would come to be associated with the act of giving one's life in the struggle against the unbelievers for the advancement of Islam (2003: 282). This idea reverses the more common notion of martyrdom associated, for example, with early Christians who were systematically killed by hostile authorities or Shia martyrs (especially Husayn) who were massacred in 680 at Karbala. Both of these latter instances reflect the choice to die rather than renounce one's faith—a defensive rather than offensive action. Without using the word martyr (*shahid*), the Qur'an does speak about those who are killed while fighting for God's cause, and several verses appear to imply that these individuals will receive a great reward (3:157-158, 4:74), although the exact nature of this reward is unclear.

Maher Jarrar indicates that the term *houris*, meaning white skinned women, is used in the Qur'an to denote what have come to be identified as the virgins of Paradise (2002: 456). The word appears four times (44:54, 52:20, 55:72, 56:22) and in three of these instances it appears with a related term meaning wide eyed. Three other verses, which do not use the term *houri*, but are linked conceptually to these discussions of rewards in Paradise, speak of women, or spouses, of modest gaze (37:48-49, 38:52, 55:56). Theories about the origin of the term and its interpretation have invoked elements of Zoroastrian mythology and postulated etymological links to a Syriac word meaning white grapes—considered to be the perfect fruit. However, beyond the fact that they are mentioned in the Qur'an among the rewards of Paradise, everything else about them is mere speculation, including the number promised, which is listed in various sources as two, seventy-two, five hundred or even eight thousand (Jarrar 2002: 457). Further, based on the content of the verses in which these beings are mentioned, they are designated as a reward for righteous behaviour, along with a host of other delights that would appeal to desert-dwelling peoples. The identification of the *houris* as a reward for martyrs has no basis in the Qur'an, however, the idea was established as early as the second Islamic century, especially among small elite groups of ascetic warriors. Its widespread use as an inducement for a person to take their own life as a means of taking the lives of others, in God's cause, is a much more recent phenomenon.

Nerina Rustomji demonstrates how the association of the *houri* with terrorism is used especially in American mainstream and social media to portray Islam as a religion characterized by sensuality, violence and irrationality (2007). She points out that evidence for the global popularity of this myth can be found in one of the infamous Danish newspaper cartoons in which Muhammad is depicted shouting to suicide bombers to stop trying to enter heaven because they have run out of virgins (79).

The word *houri* entered the English language in the early 18th century, not through the Qur'an, but from French translations of Persian mythological texts where the word was used to mean something like celestial females. Once it was part of the English lexicon, it started taking on more romantic overtones in the early part of the 19th century, for example, in the poetry of Lord Byron, developing a particularly exotic caste in Sir Walter Scott's 1819 historical novel *Ivanhoe*. At one point in the novel, Prince John asks Isaac the Jew whether Rebecca "that Eastern *houri* that thou lockest under thy arm," is his wife or his daughter. Reinforcing the clearly sexual tone of the Prince's inquiry, Rebecca, who is Isaac's daughter, is described as follows:

> Her form was exquisitely symmetrical, and was shown to advantage by a sort of Eastern dress, which she wore according to the fashion of the females of her nation. Her turban of yellow silk suited well the darkness of complexion. The brilliancy of her eyes, the superb arch of her eyebrows, her well-formed aquiline nose, her teeth as white as pearl, and the profusion of her sable tresses, which, each arranged in its own little spiral of twisted curls, fell down upon as much of a lovely neck and bosom as a simarrre of the richest Persian silk, exhibiting flowers in their natural colours embossed upon a purple ground, permitted to be visible—all these constituted a combination of loveliness, which yielded not to the most beautiful maidens who surrounded her. (qtd. in Rustomji 2007: 81-82)

It was this vision of *houris* that came to dominate English-language literary, and later theatrical and film, tradition, eventually merging with a growing, and yet sadly partial and highly selective, understanding of Islam. As Rustomji explains: "Islamic motifs are used as a way to represent a sensuality that American society enjoys, but refuses to claim as its own" (85). Because American values reflect a puritanical Christian sensibility that envisions Paradise as "a realm of spirituality, not of materialism, and certainly not of sex" (82), I would suggest that the continued fascination with the myth of the seventy-two virgins sustains America's dualistic response to terrorism, marked equally by rampant paranoia and puerile eroticism.

The direct association of the *houris* with virginity appears to be a product of the 20th century, emerging primarily in popular Arabic eschatological pamphlets (Rustomji 2007: 81). The fact that an urban legend has been co-opted in the service of religious ideology is neither surprising nor particularly innovative. The potentially sad irony of the situation, however, resides in the fact that the prize which jihadists now hold up as their greatest reward was very likely handed to them as just another part of the package of supposedly morally-bankrupt Western ideals they are seeking so desperately to undermine.

Hypocrites

Introduction

The word hypocrite has its origins in Classical Greek, where it is used to designate an actor—someone who is playing a part, a pretender. Camilla Adang points out that the Arabic term used in the Qur'an to express this idea was originally used in a literal sense to signify a tunnel or the burrow of a rat, but it also came to be applied in an attributive sense to those who were reluctant to pay the obligatory tax used to support the Muslim community in Madina (2002: 468). Combining these senses then, hypocrites came to be viewed as those who hide their true beliefs and whose actions do not match their words. While determining the rights of hypocrites in this life and their fate in the next life continues to be actively debated by Muslim scholars, for the most part the attitude towards them is one of outright hostility and condemnation.

According to al-Basri (d. 728), the gravest sinners are to be found not among the believers or unbelievers, but among the hypocrites, seemingly because, as might be stated colloquially, they lack the courage of their convictions (Adang

2002: 470). Within Islam, the term has become a general epithet with which to label one's religious opponents, with some contemporary Muslim commentators identifying groups as diverse as Freemasons, the Rotary Club and Jehovah's Witnesses as hypocrites, ostensibly because they "take their orders from the Jews" (471).

Just as hypocrisy is distinct from belief and unbelief, it is also distinct from apostasy and blasphemy. In the Qur'an, apostates are defined as "those who reject God after believing in Him" (16:106). Apostasy became a major problem in the years immediately following the death of Muhammad, when several Arabian communities chose to sever their ties with the broader Islamic community, primarily on the basis of their refusal to give funds for charity to a central authority. In an effort to quell these uprisings, Muslim armies entered into a number of battles, which collectively have come to be known as the wars of apostasy. The number of casualties was small and these wars might better be viewed as policing actions. The extent to which these rebellions against Islam and the authority of the successors to Muhammad to rule the broader Muslim community were based on religious rather than political grounds is an open question (Hallaq 2001: 121).

Turning again to the Qur'an, a blasphemer is described as someone "who invents a lie about God" (11:18), or who fails to recognize God's signs, or who associates others with God (Stewart 2001: 235). While these different expressions might appear to represent subtle variations on the theme of lack of commitment to Islam, they help us to understand that the early adoption of Islam was a gradual process, with plenty of backsliding, and the Qur'an does not attempt to eliminate or gloss over these aspects.

The material in this chapter covers the range of responses to God reflected in the Qur'an, beginning with an exploration of what constitutes true belief and orthodox practice—the religion of Islam. The next section examines those groups most closely related to the Muslims, generally referred to as the People of the Book, of whom the two most obvious representatives are the Jews and the Christians, but also including the Sabians and Magians. This is followed by a discussion of the idolaters and, because images play such an important role in idolatry, the section also includes a brief exploration of attitudes towards representational art in Islam. The next section deals with the subject of intoxication, which not only provides one of the clearest examples of abrogation in the Qur'an, it also provides an opportunity to explore Islamic attitudes towards music and dancing, both of which are often associated with Sufism, especially with respect to the practices of the Mevlevi Sufis—so-called whirling dervishes. The final topic in this chapter, and the one that brings the book as a whole to a close, is more theologically focused, and serves to highlight one of the primary sources of disagreement between Muslims and Christians—the crucifixion of Jesus. The remainder of this opening section is devoted to a further elaboration of the concept of hypocrites.

THERE ARE direct references to hypocrites in thirty verses in the Qur'an, six of which appear in the fourth surah
(4:61, 88, 138, 140, 142, 145). The first of these instances
(4:61) might be viewed as an example of concatenation, in
that it precedes the Battle Block and poses the question to
the Prophet of whether he has considered the fate of those
who turn away from God's revelation. The second instance
(4:88) occurs within the Battle Block and explicitly addresses
what is to be done with the hypocrites. As discussed more
fully in the previous chapter, this verse suggests that if the
hypocrites turn against the Prophet, then the believers are to
seize them and kill them. The last four references occur quite
close together and demonstrate a more eschatological focus,
outlining the fate of the hypocrites in the afterlife—the lowest depths of Hell (4:145).

Surah 63 is referred to as *The Hypocrites*, likely based on
the fact that it contains a succinct and yet powerful discussion of this group in its first four verses, the first three of
which state:

> When the hypocrites come to you [Prophet], they say,
> "We bear witness that you are the Messenger of God."
> God knows that you truly are His Messenger and He
> bears witness that the hypocrites are liars—they use their
> oathes as a cover and so bar others from God's way: what
> they have been doing is truly evil—because they pro-
> fessed faith and then rejected it, so their hearts have been
> sealed and they do not understand. (63:1-3)

The first verse indicates how these individuals behave
in public, with the second verse suggesting why they act
this way. The striking feature of the first verse is the use of

the expression to bear witness, which as will be explained more fully in the section on the believers mimics the declaration of faith that constitutes the first of the five pillars of Islam. As Mir indicates, it is not up to humans to verify the fact that Muhammad is God's Prophet (2008: 190). The hollow oath of the hypocrites is contrasted with the fact that God knows them to be liars. The second verse explains that they present themselves as believers in order to avoid criticism and maintain their status in the community. Reflecting the same sort of imagery as some of the uses of the concept of hijab, the third verse explains that God has sealed their hearts so that they are no longer capable of understanding the truth.

The fourth verse stands out as an excellent example of the compositional sophistication and rhetorical power of the Qur'an. Mir divides the verse into eight parts (for internal consistency I use Abdel Haleem's translation rather than Mir's):

1. When you see them [Prophet], their outward appearance pleases you;
2. when they speak, you listen to what they say.
3. But they are like propped-up timbers—
4. they think every cry they hear is against them—
5. and they are the enemy.
6. Beware of them.
7. May God confound them.
8. How devious they are!

The first two parts suggest that the hypocrites project a striking physical appearance and that they are able to charm crowds with their eloquence. The next two parts counter this impression by suggesting that in fact these individuals are soulless and artificial, afraid of every harsh word they hear, with the fifth part signifying their true identity. The next two parts outline that, as a consequence, believers should be on guard against them and that God will deal with them. Mir observes that the form and content of the final statement indicate that their behaviour is viewed as a perversion of reason and, at the same time, that it invokes elements of both surprise and regret at their state (2008: 191).

As a means of finishing off this introduction and providing a transition to the next section, the following passage illustrates the contrast between the hypocrites and the believers with respect to their reception of the Qur'an.

> When a sura is revealed, some [hypocrites] say, "Have any of you been strengthened in faith by it?" It certainly does strengthen the faith of those who believe and they rejoice, but, as for the perverse at heart, each new sura adds further to their perversity. They die disbelieving. Can they not see that they are afflicted once or twice a year? Yet they neither repent nor take heed. Whenever a sura is revealed, they look at each other and say, "Is anyone watching you?" and then they turn away—God has turned their hearts away because they are people who do not use their reason. (9:124-127)

The final verse of this passage contains an important statement about the nature of Islam. In contrast to many contemporary humanist, secularist and atheist arguments about the incompatibility of faith and reason, according to the Qur'an, it is the application of reason that leads to faith.

※   ※

Believers

The fundamental beliefs of Islam are set out in the declaration of faith (see below), as belief in the one God and belief that Muhammad is the messenger of God (Adang 2001: 219). Beyond this, however, Muslims are expected to engage in a specific set of ritual practices on a regular basis. It is because of this orientation toward the practical side of religion that, in contrast to Christianity, Islam is referred to as an orthopraxy rather than an orthodoxy. In other words, there is a greater emphasis on conformity to ritual practice than on adherence to a uniform set of beliefs. As they live their lives, according to the Qur'an, people are to respond to God with "gratitude, awe, repentance and submission" and their interactions with other people are to be characterized by "chastity, modesty, humility, forgiveness and truthfulness" (219).

A person who chooses to convert to Islam must simply recite the declaration of faith in front of two Muslim witnesses. The matter is far from that simple, however, because the burden of that declaration involves the commitment to live in accordance with the requirements set out in the five pillars (outlined below), and fulfilling this commitment takes time. The progressive nature of becoming a Muslim is highlighted in verse 49:14, in which certain Arab converts are criticized for saying that they have faith. They are instructed to say rather that they have submitted (*islam*)—faith (*iman*) will come later, as it takes time for it to enter the heart.

A more elaborate statement of what constitutes belief in Islam is provided in the so-called hadith of Gabriel, where, in response to an inquiry from a stranger, Muhammad indicates that true belief means belief in God, His angels, His books, His messengers, the Day of Judgment and fate (Murata and Chittick 1994: xxv). According to tradition, the stranger turns out to be the angel Gabriel and the responses given by the Prophet are seen to constitute both a test of his understanding of what God has revealed to him, as well as a succinct statement of what constitutes the religion of Islam.

The first verse of the fourth surah begins with the phrase, "People, be mindful of your Lord," which has often also been translated as "Mankind, fear your Lord" (Arberry 1996). The idea being referred to as both mindfulness and fear is expressed in Arabic as *taqwa*. As Alexander explains, it makes far more sense to understand this concept as referring to a state of reverence and awareness of the divine rather than one of existential anxiety, suggesting that this is the only way to make sense of a verse like 47:17, where awareness of God (*taqwa*) is a reward for following the straight path (Alexander 2002: 195). It is difficult to imagine fear as a reward for faithfulness. Turning again to the hadith of Gabriel, Murata and Chittick explain that the notion of *taqwa* is perhaps best described by this instruction from the hadith: "worship God as if you see Him, for if you do not see Him, He sees you" (1994: 267).

Based on his understanding of particular verses in the Qur'an, al-Baydawi (d. 1316) developed a three-stage model of how *taqwa* manifests itself in the life of the believer (Alexander 2002: 195). The first stage involves avoiding punishment by not attributing others to God (48:26). The second involves avoiding everything sinful, even minor offences (7:96), and the third consists of renouncing the world and devoting your entire life to God (3:102). This graduated process reflects a transition in a person's relationship with God from one of eschatological fear to one of holistic embodiment.

Elsewhere in the fourth surah (4:125), as well as in seven other verses, Muslims are instructed to follow the "religion of Abraham." All told, Abraham is referred to in 245 verses in the Qur'an, second only to the number of verses dedicated to stories about Moses. The most frequently recounted story about Abraham in the Qur'an, which has no parallel in the Torah, concerns his smashing of pagan idols and denouncing the religion of his father (e.g., 6:74-84, 29:16-27, 43:26-27). One critical sequence in these verses (6:75-79) describes how Abraham discovered monotheism through logical reasoning and the direct observation of nature. On the basis of this story, as well as from other clues such as references to Abraham as the friend of God (4:125) and as *hanif* (upright/pure of faith, e.g., 2:135, 4:125, 16:120), scholars have speculated that some form of Abrahamic monotheism existed in Arabia prior to the time of Muhammad (Firestone 2001: 6).

The more familiar story about Abraham, at least to those coming from a Jewish or Christian background, regards the extent to which he was willing to obey the commands of God—even to the point of offering up his own son as a sacrifice (37:99-111). The issue of which son, Isaac or Ishmael, was offered up continues to fuel debate in some circles, and Muslim commentators through the centuries have been split on this matter, with many ultimately deciding that the specific identity of the son is not as important as extolling the virtuous actions of the father (Firestone 2001: 10). We might surmise then that the advice to follow the religion of Abraham is a matter of applying personal reason and paying attention to what one observes in the world around them, with the result that one's natural inclination will be to submit to God.

> People, convincing proof has come to you from your Lord and We have sent a clear light down to you. God will admit those who believe in Him and hold fast to Him into His mercy and favour; He will guide them towards Him on a straight path. (4:174-175)

These two verses constitute what might be considered the theological climax of the fourth surah, in that they bring together the notions of essence and existence, through the respective images of a clear light and a straight path.

When light is referred to in the Qur'an, it usually means something like a new state of being as one moves from darkness into light (e.g., 2:257, 5:16, 14:1, 33:43), which in a literal sense signifies the difference between being blind and having sight, and in a metaphorical sense refers to the transition from ignorance to knowledge (Elias 2003: 187). When light is referred to on its own, particularly as a clear light, it means a beacon or source, as best represented by the prophetic message made available to all through the revelation of the Qur'an.

While verses that could be classified as overtly spiritual or metaphysical in content are relatively rare, one of the most famous verses in the Qur'an, and the one that can undoubtedly be considered its most esoteric, is the Light Verse.

God is the Light of the heavens and the earth. His Light is like this: there is a niche, and in it a lamp, the lamp inside a glass, a glass like a glittering star, fuelled from a blessed olive tree from neither east nor west, whose oil almost gives light even when no fire touches it—light upon light—God guides whoever He will to his Light; God draws such comparisons for people; God has full knowledge of everything. (24:35)

As with verses 4:174-175, the Light Verse couples the metaphysical imagery of light with the practical idea of guidance. The project of interpreting the Light Verse over the centuries has given rise to a distinct genre of spiritual literature in Islam, especially among Sufis and in the Persian Islamic philosophical tradition known as illuminationism, which is associated mainly with the works of Suhrawardi (d. 1168) and Mulla Sadra (d. 1640).

Several different Arabic words are used in the Qur'an to signify a path, but when the word *sirat* is used, as in 4:175, it is used exclusively to mean "the way of God" (Frolov 2004: 28). Michael Cook notes that the word *sirat* has no plural in Arabic, thus reinforcing the impression that the path laid out by the Qur'an is unique or perfect (2000: 9). Some scholars have suggested that the word is derived from the Latin word *strata*, meaning a layer, or to stretch out, but, as Frolov points out, its use in Arabic was unknown prior to the Qur'an (2004: 28).

The linkage of guidance to the idea of God's path in 4:175 is particularly significant because it parallels the sixth verse of the first surah (*The Opening*): "Guide us on the straight path," which is the only actual request made of God by believers.

The five pillars of Islam, which articulate the details of the straight path, include the declaration of faith (*shahadah*), performing prayer (*salat*) five times per day, giving alms (*zakat*), fasting (*sawm*) during the month of Ramadan, and making the pilgrimage (*hajj*) to Makkah once in your life, if you have the means to do so.

With the declaration of faith a Muslim bears witness that there is no god but God and that Muhammad is the messenger of God (Rippin 2006). There is no direct statement of this declaration in the Qur'an, but its various elements occur in several verses. Unlike a creedal statement, the idea of bearing witness (2:143, 3:64) suggests more than the simple articulation of beliefs. Viewed as a practice, it implies that the way in which people live their lives will attest to those beliefs. Monotheism is the central theological message of the Qur'an (2:255, 37:35, 47:19) and thus the first part of the declaration serves to differentiate Muslims from idolaters and polytheists.

In the second part, Muslims differentiate themselves from other monotheists through the recognition of the prophethood of Muhammad (7:158, 48:29, 49:3). This part of the declaration is often explained as capturing the idea that while there have been other prophets prior to Muhammad he is the last and final prophet—the "seal of the prophets" (33:40). In recognition of the imamate and especially as a reflection of their belief that Ali was the rightful successor to Muhammad, the Shia often add a third component to the declaration indicating that Ali is the friend of God (Momen 1985: 147-60).

Prayer is mentioned continuously in the Qur'an, but the precise instructions regarding when and how prayer is to be performed are only spelled out later in the hadith literature. One of the principle features of Islamic prayer is the recitation of the first surah (*The Opening*), which devout Muslims will say seventeen times throughout the day, and which some scholars think was deliberately composed to serve as the basis for communal prayer (Böwering 2004: 221). Precedents for the physical postures associated with prayer, such as standing (2:238), bowing (2:43) and prostration (4:102), all appear in the Qur'an, as does the instruction to include recitation of sections of the Qur'an as part of prayer (17:78, 35:29).

Once the Islamic community was firmly established in Madina, the direction of prayer was shifted from Jerusalem to Makkah (2:142-150), in part to differentiate Muslims from their Jewish neighbours and in part to recognize the sacred status of Makkah. With respect to the times of day at which prayer is to be performed, the Qur'an stipulates the morning and evening (6:52, 18:28), as well as a middle prayer (2:238). Night prayers are mentioned most specifically with reference to religious obligations incumbent on the Prophet (73:20). Böwering suggests that the traditional five times that became established (sunrise, mid-day, mid-afternoon, sunset and evening) represent a middle way between the three observed by the Jews and the seven practised by Christian monks (2004: 228). Interestingly, while the Shia perform the five obligatory prayers, by combining the noon and afternoon prayers and the evening and night prayers, they reduce the actual performance times of prayer throughout the day to three (Momen 1985: 178).

Several verses address prayer-related issues. For example, women are specifically instructed to pray (33:33), thus making them no different from men with respect to this obligation. Travellers are permitted to shorten their prayers (4:101), and those in danger are allowed to pray while walking or riding (2:239). Two preparatory steps are outlined, the first of which is the instruction for ritual purification through cleansing with water (4:43, 5:6), or the use of clean sand when water is not available. The second step is the public call to prayer (5:58), which is to be done by the human voice as opposed to a horn, bell or some other mechanical means.

Outside of the formal obligatory prayers, Muslims also perform a variety of personal supplications, but irrespective of whatever form it takes, the Qur'an is always central to both the idea and practice of prayer.

> In the experience of the Muslim, God speaks to human
> beings through the Qur'an and human beings, reciting the
> Qur'an, address themselves to God. (Böwering 2004: 230)

With respect to almsgiving, Azim Nanji explains that the Qur'an establishes a framework for sharing resources through giving, in that it makes no distinction between material and spiritual pursuits for humanity, it envisions the Islamic community as seeking the good and struggling against evil, and it regards Muslims as trustees of wealth and property (2001: 64). A distinction is made between voluntary (*sadaqa*) and obligatory (*zakat*) giving, but both are seen as a means of seeking God's pleasure and earning rewards in the afterlife. Hoarders of wealth are condemned (3:180).

With respect to the distribution of alms, eight categories of recipients are identified in the following verse:

> Alms are meant only for the poor, the needy, those who
> administer them, those whose hearts need winning over,
> to free slaves and help those in debt, for God's cause, and
> for travelers in need. This is ordained by God; God is all
> knowing and wise. (9:60)

It is worth noting, perhaps as a reflection of the mercan-
tile culture of the Makkans, that this verse recognizes that
there are costs associated with the collection and distribution of donations. Also, despite the fact that Muslims did not
actively seek conversions among outsiders, this verse allows
for donations to be used to support the growth of the Islamic community, likely from the ranks of the local population, especially kinfolk, through conversion. Many would
suggest that it also permits the use of gifts for defence of the
community against its opponents (God's cause). Giving does
not necessarily have to take the form of money or material
goods, but can consist of volunteer work (9:79) or offering a
kind word (2:263). Finally, consistent with the fact that giving is done to please God, charity should be done discreetly
rather than for public acknowledgement (2:271).

The obligation to fast during the month of Ramadan
captures two distinct elements—fasting and the recognition of a particular time of year as possessing special religious significance. Kees Wagtendonk indicates that three
kinds of fasting are recognized in the Qur'an: ritual fasting during Ramadan, which involves abstaining from food,
drink and sexual activity during daylight hours; compensa-
tory fasting, in which brief periods of fasting can be used as

a form of repentance or payback for breaking an oath (58:3-4), unintentional manslaughter (4:92), or failing to follow certain pilgrimage rules (2:196); and fasting as an ascetic practice (2002: 180-81). Ritual fasting for the Muslims is generally thought to have begun when Muhammad and his followers reached Madina and observed the Jews fasting on Yom Kippur (Day of Atonement). Apparently the Prophet's instruction for his people to fast on this day was based on his perception of Moses as his predecessor, in bringing a message to his people and acting as God's agent in delivering them from some form of bondage (2002: 182). The practice of fasting was then extended to cover a set period of days (most often thought to be ten), and then finally to encompass the entire month of Ramadan. The institution of the ritual is laid out in a sequence of verses (2:183-186), with the instructions for the longer period set out in verse 185 seen as an abrogation of the shorter period set out in verse 184.

The recognition of Ramadan as a holy month has precedents in the observance of the Jewish Passover, Christian Easter and a pre-Islamic Arab seasonal festival (*umra*), all of which have roots in agricultural and religious observances of sacrifice and thanksgiving (Neuwirth 2004: 338-40). Along with fasting, Ramadan is devoted to the commemoration of the revelation of the Qur'an, with the entire Qur'an being recited over the thirty days. The performance of this ritual reflects the fact that Muhammad is said to have received his first revelation while on a spiritual retreat during this month, and one night in particular, the Night of Power or Night of Destiny (*laylat al-qadr*), is mentioned (44:3, 97:1), possibly marking the actual night of the first revelation, or at least signifying a time when communication between heaven and Earth was thought to flow more easily (Neuwirth 2004: 342).

The final pillar of Islam is the obligation to make the pilgrimage to Makkah once in your lifetime, if you have the means to do so. As Hawting explains, based on the etymology of the words used to describe it, the ritual appears to have less to do with travelling to Makkah than it does with movement (circumambulation/dance/procession) around the Ka'ba and other specific sites (2004: 92). The Qur'an (2:196-209) mentions a major pilgrimage (*hajj*), which tradition has held to be obligatory, and a minor pilgrimage (*umra*), which is considered an optional act of devotion. It is clear from the way in which this ritual is referred to in the Qur'an that many of the particulars are pre-Islamic, and the verses are primarily concerned with assuring Muslims that certain elements of the ritual are in fact consistent with Islam.

The historicity of the ritual is further attested by the mention of specific locations around Makkah, such as Safa and Marwa (2:158), two hills near the Ka'ba, and Arafat, a hill about twenty-five kilometers east of Makkah (2:198). The complexity of the ritual and the regulations surrounding its performance have increased over the centuries, but, as Murata and Chittick suggest, in the days before "steamships, airplanes and buses," performing the pilgrimage could take a year or more out of a person's life, and it was viewed by the pilgrim and others as a life-altering experience (1994: 19-20).

As a final note related to the pilgrimage, Muslims consider the Ka'ba to be the most sacred spot on Earth (Hawting 2003: 75). The structure is directly mentioned only twice in the Qur'an, in closely located verses (5:95, 97), both of which allude to its role as a sanctuary. It is often described as a cube, but it is about 40 feet long, 33 feet wide and 50 feet high, with a large black stone built into its eastern corner. Both the major and minor pilgrimages begin and end with circumambulations of the Ka'ba, during which pilgrims attempt to touch the black stone.

Some scholars have speculated that the stone is in fact a meteorite that fell in this area, with the shrine being constructed to commemorate its impact (Thomsen 1980). Muslims all around the world face the Ka'ba when they pray, as well as during the performance of other rituals, such as slaughtering animals for food. Two other closely located verses (2:125, 127) tell how Abraham and Ishmael were instructed to rebuild God's house for those who would worship there. The interpretation of these verses is linked to a tradition that associates the Ka'ba with the place that Adam prayed after his exile from the garden, but which, with the exception of its foundation, had been destroyed during Noah's flood (Firestone 2001: 9).

Among the unbelievers, Adang points out that they either are polytheists, idolaters or hypocrites (2001: 221). The Qur'an does not really recognize any group that we might label as atheists (Mir 2004). Muslims are forbidden to sit with those unbelievers who mock the Qur'an (4:140) and several verses (e.g., 4:144, 5:51, 13:1, 60:1) suggest that those believers who associate with unbelievers are counted as one of them. In one verse (9:28), the unbelievers are declared to be impure and this has led in some instances to the development of laws prohibiting non-Muslims from visiting Islamic holy sites and places of worship.

There are several verses (e.g., 17:15, 20:82, 39:41) in the Qur'an that suggest that individuals have control over their fate in the afterlife, but there are a greater number of verses (e.g., 6:125, 13:33, 39:23, 74:31) which indicate that a person's fate has already been decided by God (Adang 2001: 225). This apparent contradiction has given rise to theological arguments about free will and determinism, with some groups suggesting that absolute determinism is inconsistent with the concept of divine justice. On the other hand, unbelievers are described as those whose hearts and ears have been sealed (45:23, 63:3).

※　※

People of the Book

The expression "People of the Book" is used in the Qur'an primarily in a pejorative and polemical sense to refer to the Jews and the Christians (Sharon 2004: 36). More generally, however, it is used to refer to all those who have received a book from God through the mediation of a messenger (e.g., 2:145, 3:19, 4:131, 5:5, 6:20). Certain books are mentioned by name—the Torah (*tawrat*) given to Moses (7:145, 62:5), the Gospel (*injil*) of Jesus (57:27) and the Psalms (*zabur*) given to David (4:163, 17:55). Other books are alluded to but not named (87:18-19). While all of these books are considered to be the word of God, the two principle recipients of these earlier books, namely, the Jews and the Christians, are seen to have veered away from the messages they were sent in two ways. First, they concealed or changed the message (2:174, 4:46, 5:13). Second, they failed to see the truth of the book now being delivered through Muhammad (5:19, 6:91-92). Thus, while we might view the Muslims as People of Book, the expression "People of the Qur'an" became common in the hadith literature, as a means of designating those who, in following the Qur'an, had now truly become the people of the book. Those Jews and the Christians who did not accept the validity of the Qur'an would now be counted among the polytheists.

Throughout Islam's history, the assignation "People of the Book" would be used positively and negatively, as religious and political circumstances changed. For example, it appears that during the reign of the Mughal emperor Akbar (1542-1605) the category was even extended to include Hindus (Küng 2007: 399). In this respect the term became a means of designating those religions that were considered legitimate, thus allowing followers to worship freely. While it is beyond the scope of the present discussion, the debate over the extent to which the Qur'an advocates a position of tolerance towards other religions and the extent to which Muslims in today's world should acknowledge and accept religious pluralism continues unabated (Sachedina 2001; Wilde and McAuliffe 2004).

The Qur'an continuously refers to itself as a book (e.g., 2:2, 4:105, 6:92, 7:2, 16:89, 39:23). Daniel Madigan points out that all but a few of the 261 occurrences of the word *kitab* in the Qur'an refer specifically to the word of God and thus it makes sense to translate *kitab* as scripture rather than book (2001: 243). He goes on to explain that in an overarching sense the book is a repository of divine knowledge, which in the case of the Qur'an manifests itself in two ways. First it is an inventory of all that God has created, and thus a means through which people can gain a clear understanding of all things. Second it is a record of the deeds of every individual in preparation for the accounting that will take place on the Day of Judgment. However, this documentary aspect is balanced with a more active role as a revelation, such that when God sent messengers to the people they were sent with a book (2:213, 3:81, 35:25, 40:70, 57:25). Among the specific peoples related to these books, the Qur'an identifies the Sabian, Magians, Jews, Christians and finally the Muslims.

As François de Blois points out, the Sabians, who are mentioned three times in the Qur'an (2:62, 5:69, 22:17), are not to be confused with the Sabaeans (2004: 511). This latter term designates the people of the Queen of Sheba, whose story is related in a sequence of verses (34:15-21) in an eponymous surah (*Sheba*). As for the Sabians, little scholarly consensus exists as to their identity, but de Blois suggests that they could be Manichaeans—members of a Gnostic sect with a highly dualistic cosmology that emerged in Persia towards the end of the 3rd century. This sect spread rapidly throughout the Roman Empire as well as eastward and had a significant influence on the development of Christian theology.

In one of these verses (22:17), the Magians, normally thought to be Zoroastrians, are also mentioned. William Darrow points out that while the Magians are most often identified as a professional priesthood of fire-worshippers from Persia, the primary focus of commentary on this verse has not been so much on positively identifying this group, but rather on the issue of whether the listing of the various forms of religion should be interpreted as a ranking along a continuum, with the unbelievers (polytheists/atheists) on one end and the believers (Muslims) on the other (Darrow 2003: 244-45). If a spectrum of belief is intended, then it is instructive to observe that those closest to the Muslims in belief are the Jews, followed by the Sabians and then the Christians.

With so much of the content of the Qur'an paralleling the stories and personalities found in the Torah, it might appear that the Qur'an has a great deal to say about the Jews. For the most part, however, when the Qur'an specifically mentions the Jews, the references are to people living at or near the time of the Prophet. Accounts of events relating to Abraham, Moses, Noah and Lot, for example, should more accurately be viewed as referring to the predecessors of the Jews, some of whom were exemplary in their righteousness (e.g., Abraham) and others who stand out as ultimate sinners (e.g., Lot's people). The fate of these groups, whether positive or negative, is unambiguously presented in the Qur'an. The same, however, cannot be said about the fate of the Jews. While in some verse they are recognized as believers (e.g., 2:62, 4:162, 5:69), elsewhere, they are condemned for twisting the words of scripture (4:46) and for taking usury (4:160-161). As Rubin explains, the shifting attitude towards the Jews represented throughout the Qur'an likely reflects the growing tension between the Muslims and their Jewish neighbours in Madina, as Islam gained in strength, religious and political (2003: 33-34).

Rubin indicates that several verses in the Qur'an (e.g., 7:103-133, 44:30-33, 45:16-17) refer to the Children of Israel (2001: 303). These passages focus on the idea that the Israelites were chosen by God as a special community that was delivered from bondage in Egypt, but then because they chose to worship the golden calf and commit other sins, they eventually lost their status. Rubin suggests that this designation is used in the Qur'an as a means of differentiating between the original faithful followers of God and the Jews and Christians living at the time of the Prophet (305). Both of these latter groups were seen to have gone astray, with the Muslims now replacing the Israelites as God's chosen people.

According to Sidney Griffith, the people often referred to as Christians in translations of the Qur'an should more accurately be referred to as Nazarenes, as the Arabic word being translated as Christians is actually *nasara*, ostensibly based on the fact that Jesus was thought to have been born in Nazareth (2001: 310). There had been Christians in Arabia right back to the 1st century, as evidenced in the New Testament book Galatians (1:17) where Paul indicates that he travelled to Arabia after his conversion for a period of contemplation, and certainly by the time of the Prophet Christian communities were well established in the peninsula. However, the standard Arabic word for Christians (*masihiyyun*) never appears in the Qur'an, with Griffith suggesting that this might reflect a particular polemical strategy, namely, a mechanism for positively identifying this group while at the same time implicitly denying that Jesus was the messiah (2001: 314). This matter remains largely unexplored.

References to specific aspects of Christianity are very few in the Qur'an, but one idea that does receive attention is the doctrine of the Trinity.

> Those people who say that God is the third of three are defying [the truth]: there is only One God. (5:73)

> So believe and God and His messengers and do not speak of a "Trinity"—stop [this], that is better for you—God is only One God. (4:171)

The Christian doctrine of the Trinity has a complex history, beginning more than two centuries after the death of Jesus, as theologians attempted to elaborate on the nature—divine or human—of Jesus and the action of God in the world (Thomas 2006). The doctrine became embedded in the creed (statement of belief) established at the Council of Nicaea in 325, and from there became the continued subject of scholarly debate, best represented in the works of Boethius (d. 524) and Aquinas (d. 1274). The essential elements of the doctrine are that the one God exists in three persons (Father, Son and Holy Spirit). Within the Church, disagreements over the way in which the Trinity is described in the creed were instrumental in leading to the separation in 1054 between the Roman Catholic Church in the West and the Orthodox Churches in the East. The so-called *filioque* clause in the creed suggests that the Holy Spirit emanates from the Father and the Son, whereas the Eastern churches argued that both the Son and the Holy Spirit must emanate solely from the Father, the single and only creator of all things.

Within Islam, the doctrine is viewed as *shirk*—the association of others with God, thus rendering Christianity a polytheistic religion. It is critical to a proper understanding of the Qur'an and Islam to remember that, even though Christians are most often portrayed as hypocrites or polytheists, Jesus is highly revered. Along with Noah, Abraham, Moses and Muhammad, Jesus is considered one of the five major prophets of Islam. His status and mission are stated clearly in the Qur'an:

> The angels said, "Mary, God gives you news of a Word from Him, whose name will be the Messiah, Jesus, son of Mary, who will be held in honour in this world and the next, who will be one of those brought near to God. He will speak to people in his infancy and his adulthood. He will be one of the righteous." (3:45)

※　※

Idolatry

This section deals with the related issues of idolatry and polytheism, both of which are examples of what is referred to in Arabic as *shirk*, meaning to associate others with God (Hawting 2002a, 2002b; Mir 2004). According to the Qur'an (4:48 and 4:116), *shirk* is the only sin for which there is no forgiveness. As mentioned in the first chapter, these two verses display nearly identical wording, and serve to link the two intermediary sections identified by Zahniser in the fourth surah, the first of which deals mainly with the transgressions of the People of the Book, and the second of which addresses the errors of pre-Islamic Arabian idolatry.

Mir suggests that Arabic polytheism was in fact henotheism, a theological system in which multiple local deities are worshipped along with a Supreme God (2004: 160). Evidence for this assessment can be found in verse 39:3, where the people of Makkah excuse their worship of these lesser deities by saying: "We only worship them because they bring us nearer to God." However, the danger of adhering to old patterns of worship is highlighted in the story of Luqman (31:12-19), where he warns his son against the evil of attributing partners to God (31:13). In what would clearly be seen as a break with social norms, Luqman goes so far as to state that while children should respect and obey their parents, they are obliged to disobey their parents should they strive to make them believe in anything other than God (31:14-15).

There are several references to idolatry in the fourth surah, with those that occur in the first intermediary section (4:44-70) differing quite significantly from those that occur in the second (4:105-126). One verse (4:51) indicates that there are some among the People of the Book who have suggested that those who worship idols are more rightly guided than the believers. Another verse (4:60) relates that there are those who previously a message from God, who now want to turn to unjust tyrants for judgment. A third verse (4:76) suggests that those who reject faith fight for an unjust cause. The Arabic word *taghut* occurs in all three verses alternately translated as idols, tyrant and unjust cause, but its origins and intended meaning remain a mystery (Hawting 2002b: 482).

The references to idolatry in the second intermediary section are far more specific than those that occur in the first. For example, one verse (4:117) states that "the idolaters invoke only females," and another verse puts these words into the mouth of Satan:

> I will mislead them and incite vain desires in them; I will command them to slit the ears of cattle; I will command them to tamper with God's creation. (4:119)

While we can only speculate about the religious significance of the curious action regarding cattle, it is reasonable to suggest that the initial audience for the Qur'an would know exactly what was being talked about.

Among the pagan deities that are mentioned by name in the Qur'an are Wadd, Suwa, Yaghuth, Yauq and Nasr, in association with the people of Noah (71:23), along with three goddesses worshipped by the Makkans (53:19-20).

It is difficult to imagine that anyone would not be familiar with the expression "Satanic Verses," although the significance of the story regarding these verses is only peripherally associated with the still ongoing controversies surrounding the publication of the novel by that name written by Salman Rushdie (1988). The first matter to clear up is that there is no direct evidence that these verses were ever part of the Qur'an (Ahmed 2004: 531). By the beginning of the second Muslim century, however, this story began to appear in several biographical and exegetical works, and heated debates over the existence and interpretation of this story have been ongoing ever since.

In the context of what the Qur'an has to say about idolatry, the story refers to the mention of three pre-Islamic female deities known as al-Lat, al-Uzza and Manat (53:19-20). According to the traditional accounts, as Muhammad was reciting these verses to the Makkans, Satan caused him to add a statement to the effect that these are the high [flying] cranes (some say maidens), whose intercession is desired. When members of the Quraysh heard this, they interpreted it as an acknowledgement of their tribal deities and consequently they joined the Muslims in prostration at the end of the recitation. Afterwards, Gabriel came to Muhammad, informing him of his error, and offering him some reassurance, saying that Satan had interfered with the work of many prophets in the past. Immediately, Muhammad acknowledged his error and recanted the verses, which led to renewed hostilities with the Quraysh.

It was only several centuries later that the legitimacy of the story was seriously questioned, with two primary objections being raised about the historicity of this incident. First, Islamic scholars were concerned that, in acknowledging that Muhammad had been led astray in this instance, the veracity of other verses would be called into question. Second, in keeping with the accepted mechanisms for establishing the authority of the hadith literature, they were concerned that there was no definitive chain of transmission associated with the accounts of this story. Many modern non-Muslim commentators suggest that there must be some historical basis for the story, because, as Francis Peters expresses it, "it is impossible to imagine a Muslim inventing such an inauspicious tale" (qtd. in Ahmed 2004: 535). While the Rushdie affair has added fuel to ceaseless debates about the depiction of the Muhammad in visual and literary arts, it has not rekindled discussions over the veracity of the original story.

It might seem odd that depictions of humans in art and photography are linked to idolatry, but as Leaman explains, Muslims developed a non-representational artistic style as yet another means for differentiating themselves from Jews and Christians (2004: 17-22). At the same time, he is quick to point out that: "The ban on images in Islam does not exist" (17).

> Why should there be a ban on representing even the Prophet in a picture? He was after all a human being and to suggest that he is too holy to be represented visually implies that he shares in God's divine status, which is directly in opposition to the central principles of Islam. (61)

The fact that people might associate an image with the actual presence of the divine is only part of the problem. The potential also exists for images presented in various art forms to be held up as objects of ridicule, or, in the case of pictures of women, sources of titillation. Of potentially even greater concern is the possibility of an image misrepresenting a religious act. In this regard, Abou El Fadl relates that according to Saudi jurists a moving picture of a person reciting the Qur'an is legal, but a still picture of a person reading the Qur'an is not (2001: 198). The rationale in this case would appear to be that the moving picture at least provides a mechanism through which the act of recitation can speak for itself.

※   ※

Intoxication

The way in which the subject of intoxication is dealt with in the Qur'an is instructive because it offers a clear demonstration of how the ruling on various matters changed in response to changing religious and social conditions. Further, it provides the least ambiguous, and probably the least contended, example of the process of abrogation, through which some verses are deemed to replace other verses that had been revealed earlier dealing with the same or similar subject matter.

That the Arabs enjoyed beverages made from the fruits they had available to them is stated explicitly in the Qur'an.

> From the fruits of date palms and grapes you take sweet juice and wholesome provisions. (16:67)

At the same time, this verse does not explicitly suggest that these juices were fermented to produce alcohol. However, other verses, dealing with the rewards which believers will gain access to in the afterlife, establish a contrast between earthly and heavenly beverages, for example:

> [E]verlasting youths will go round among them with glasses, flagons and cups of a pure drink that causes no headaches or intoxication; (56:17-19)

At the very least, these verses suggests that the Arabs were familiar with drinks containing alcohol and that, even though there were negative effects associated with these drinks, they were held in high enough regard to be identified as a reward for righteousness—albeit in a pure form.

Enes Karic explains that wine was the main intoxicant throughout the Middle East and Mediterranean, playing a prominent role in several stories within Jewish and Christian scripture, and taking on special significance when it was incorporated into the Christian liturgy of the Eucharist (2002: 556). She notes that the etymology of the Arabic word *khamr*, which is translated as wine, originally meant "something which covers the mind" (557). While it is very likely an exaggeration to suggest that the association of wine with the divine and transformative nature of Jesus contributed to the initial sanctions against its use in the Qur'an, it is reasonable to propose that some aspect of this association would have become part of the rhetorical arsenal employed in efforts to justify and enforce the prohibition as Islam matured and spread.

With respect to the progressive nature of the prohibition, the three relevant verses are presented here in their purported order of revelation.

> They ask you [Prophet] about intoxicants and gambling: say "There is great sin in both, and some benefit for people: the sin is greater than the benefit." (2:219)

> You who believe, do not come anywhere near the prayer if you are intoxicated, not until you know what you are saying; (4:43)

> You who believe, intoxicants and gambling, idolatrous practices, and divining with arrows are repugnant acts— Satan's doing—shun them so that you may prosper. With intoxicants and gambling, Satan seeks only to incite enmity and hatred among you, and to stop you remembering God and prayer. Will you not give them up? (5:90-91)

The initial verse in this set expresses a moral judgment, resembling a social norm aimed at discouraging behaviours that are likely to negatively impact families and the broader community. The second verse is decidedly religious in nature and links the effects of alcohol with the inability to properly carry out one's religious obligations. The final verse combines the social and religious elements of a series of behaviours, with the result that drinking alcohol not only becomes viewed as Satan's doing, but it almost appears to be equated with idolatry. As previously stated, there is little if any disagreement among Muslims that this final verse was intended to replace the initial two references, with the result that the consumption of alcohol is strictly forbidden.

In a study of contemporary alcohol consumption among Muslims in countries where they are the majority, as well as in countries where they are not, Laurence Michalak and Karen Trocki observe that irrespective of the fact that its use is forbidden, "alcohol abuse among Muslims is a significant social problem" (2006: 524). This seeming incongruity between religious regulation and social practice is not new, and there is a certain irony in the fact that Muslims in Spain refined the distillation techniques that allowed for the systematic production of spirits and that the word alcohol comes the Arabic *al-kuhul*, meaning essence. At the same time the social stigma attached to alcohol abuse is reflected well in this aphorism relayed to the authors by one of their informants in Tunis:

> Which is the worst deed: to kill a man, to rape a woman, or to get drunk? Drunkenness is the worst because the drunkard will commit both rape and murder. (524)

While the World Health Organization lists Islamic nations as having the lowest reported per capita rates of alcohol consumption in the world, the organization also stresses that evidence, such as a substantial literature on alcohol treatment in Saudi Arabia, suggests that the unreported rates are much higher (Michalak and Trocki 2006: 536). The authors mention that in highly regulated environments such as Saudi Arabia prohibition is balanced by a strong sense of the division between public and private life, resulting in a sort of "don't ask, don't tell" approach (547). By contrast, the environment in Turkey is much more permissive, with good quality beer, wine and spirits being produced locally and made available at very low prices. Interestingly, Mustafa Kemal Ataturk, the great Turkish secularist, died in 1938 from cirrhosis of the liver (548).

Among the younger generation, especially those migrating to Europe or North America, the authors identify two key groups: "fallen" Muslims who take up drinking alcohol upon arriving in an environment where this is the norm and "born again" Muslims, who are exposed to alcohol when they immigrate, begin drinking, but then reject it along with other excesses, leading them to rediscover Islam and become much stricter in their religious practice (551-52). In those instances where sufficient numbers of young Muslims have participated in studies about alcohol use, the authors observe that they more often cite health reasons rather than religious regulations as the basis for their abstention (540).

Although the earliest references to intoxication in the Qur'an, hadith literature and commentaries focus on the consumption of alcohol, and more specifically wine, opinions differ on whether the prohibition extends to other forms of alcoholic beverages (e.g., beer, distilled spirits), not to mention a host of other intoxicating or neuro-active substances such as hallucinogenic drugs, caffeine and nicotine (Karic 2002). The primary support for a broad-spectrum ban on intoxicants comes from the fact that they can interfere with the performance of religious obligations and, on a more social level, they have the potential to cause, or at least not inhibit, an individual bringing a false accusation against another person (Kamali 2003: 289). However, as Islam developed, the ban on intoxicants became more and more associated with negative judgments regarding the practices of Sufis, in particular, the Mevlevis—more commonly known as whirling dervishes (Leaman 2004: 69-73).

The Mevlevi order was founded by the Persian mystic Jalal al-Din Rumi (d. 1273), whose poetry is full of references to singing, dancing and drinking wine, although these are most often interpreted as representing means through which the devotee can come closer to God (Barks 2004). Certainly with respect to wine, for the Sufis, rather than referring to the actual drinking of alcohol, which they do not, it signifies the metaphysical act of spiritually imbibing in the divine essence—a transformative act which clearly produces an altered state of consciousness, to which anyone who has ever watched the dervishes perform can attest.

Singing and dancing are an integral part of Sufi practice and much of the criticism against these activities is based on the notion that aesthetic considerations come to take precedence over genuine devotion. Religion becomes subordinated to art. However, as Leaman states:

> They are not important because they are beautiful, they are beautiful because they are important, and they are important because they help re-attach us to God. (77)

It is intriguing to observe that the same sort of physiological response that is condemned with respect to Sufi practices is viewed as an appropriate and desirable outcome of listening to the recitation of the Qur'an.

> God has sent down the most beautiful of all teachings: a Scripture that is consistent and draws comparisons; that causes the skins of those in awe of their Lord to shiver. Then their skins and their hearts soften at the mention of God: such is God's guidance. (39:23)

Anna Gade points out that according to Islamic tradition the melody of a recitation is not be written down or fixed in any way, so that the technical vocal skills and artistry of the reciter will not overtake the inherent beauty and perfection of the word of God (2004: 380). In a sense, each new recitation is a new revelation of God's message, divinely inspired and solely a reflection of God's grace granted to the reciter. At the same time, there can be little question that the melodic patterns used by reciters reflect the influence of popular Arabic music throughout the ages. Kristina Nelson documents the style and reputation of several Egyptian reciters, who through the dissemination of their recordings have become the rock stars of the Muslim world, attracting large audiences and being treated like celebrities (2001).

As one final example of intoxication and its place in Islam, there is a long tradition among the Shia of performing passion plays on the tenth day of the month of Muharram to commemorate the martyrdom of Husayn at Karbala in 680 (Momen 1985: 240-42). The physical and spiritual intensity of that these re-enactments from a visitor to Tehran in the late 1800s:

> Men almost naked run through the city, striking their
> breasts rapidly; others piercing their arms and legs with
> knives, fastening padlocks in the flesh under their breasts,
> or making wide gashes in their heads, invoke their saints
> with frightful howlings, shouting out Hassan! Hussein!
> (qtd. in Momen 1985: 241)

※　※

The Crucifixion of Jesus

As mentioned above in the section on the People of the
Book, Jesus is considered to be one of the major prophets
of Islam. According to tradition, Jesus was taken up into
heaven by God to wait for the moment prior to the Day of
Judgment when he will return to Earth, defeat the Anti-
christ, reign over a forty-year time of peace, die of natural
causes and be buried in Madina (Robinson 2003: 17). Then,
with the arrival of the Day of Judgment Jesus will be called
upon as a witness against the unbelievers of the People of
the Book. While much of this scenario is derived from the
content of certain verses in the Qur'an, other aspects reflect the integration of material from the Christian apocalyptic tradition. However, in the Qur'an, the critical fact
about Jesus informing this whole tradition is that he was
not crucified by the Jews.

> [B]ecause they disbelieved and uttered a terrible slan-
> der against Mary, and said, "We have killed the Messiah,
> Jesus, son of Mary, the Messenger of God." They did not
> kill him, nor did they crucify him, though it was made to
> appear like that to them. Those that disagreed about him

are full of doubt, with no knowledge to follow, only sup-position: they certainly did not kill him, God raised him up to Himself. God is almighty and wise. There is not one of the People of the Book who will not believe in Jesus before his death, and on the Day of Resurrection he will be a witness against them. (4:156-159)

While Muslims have used this passage as the basis for their claim that Jesus was not crucified, Christian apolo-gists have argued that the text does not actually say that Je-sus was not crucified; rather, it merely states that it was not the Jews who carried it out (Robinson 2003: 20). As the opening portion of the following passage suggests, while there is no doubt that there was a plot to kill Jesus, God also had a plan.

The [disbelievers] schemed but God also schemed; God is the Best of Schemers. God said, "Jesus, I will take you back and raise you up to Me: I will purify you of the disbelievers. To the Day of Resurrection I will make those who follow you superior to those who disbelieved. Then you will all return to me and I will judge between you regarding your differences." (3:54-55)

Todd Lawson indicates that the coverage of the cruci-fixion in the Qur'an is in many ways more about the Jews than it is about Jesus, in that one of the major lessons to be learned from the story is that the Jews "are being con-demned for their boast that they were able to contravene the will of God by killing his prophet and messenger, Jesus the son of Mary" (2009: 27).

In the Qur'an, life and death are viewed as instruments of God's providence for humanity and, even though a person might mortally wound another, it is God who ultimately causes the person to die (Waardenburg 2001: 508). Prophets are no exception. Because life is viewed as a gift, it is to be used in God's service. In this respect prophets might be viewed as exceptional, but they are prophets because God has willed them to be so, not because they set out to become one. Irrespective of one's role, death is not the end of life, but rather the end of a period of testing, after which a person will either be rewarded or punished. In the metaphysics of the Qur'an, "the natural opposition between life and death merges into the spiritual one between belief and disbelief" (510).

RECALLING ZAHNISER'S assumption that position is hermeneutic, we might wonder about the significance of the placement within the fourth surah of the verses dealing with the crucifixion. As outlined in the final section of the first chapter, the fifth part of the surah (verses 127-176) constitutes a smaller version of the entire surah, demonstrating a parallel thematic structure: the Women Cluster (127-135), a hollow portion (136-175) and the Women Verse (176). The content of the hollow portion resembles what is contained in the two intermediary sections of the surah—material on the hypocrites, idolatry and the People of the Book. Not only are the verses on the crucifixion (156-159) contained in this sequence, but so are the verses on the Trinity (170-171). These two closely placed references to aspects of Christian doctrine might lead some readers to conclude that this portion of the surah is meant to be interpreted as a very pointed polemic against Christians. However, when this part of the surah is viewed holistically, a much broader interpretation can be suggested.

I indicated at the outset that based on my reading of the surah its three major themes are monotheism, guidance and judgment. I also indicated that one sequence of verses (137-143) in the hollow section, which Zahniser identified as a potential chiasm, appeared to focus on the idea that hypocrites and disbelievers are destined for Hell. I would propose that the highly specific references to the Trinity and the crucifixion that follow this condemnation are designed to accomplish at least three things. First, they are directed at specific subsets of the People of the Book, with the discussion of the Trinity directed at the Christians and the matter of what the crucifixion meant, as just demonstrated, for the Jews. Second, these two sequences deal with highly specific and sophisticated aspects of theology, thus in some sense meeting the opponents on their own playing fields. Third, they provide a dramatic mechanism for drawing together the three themes.

The theme of judgment is explicit in the condemnation of the hypocrites and disbelievers, but the context of eternal judgment is also balanced with the need to practice a more mundane and yet equally important form of judgment in living the everyday life of a Muslim. This component is highlighted by the fact that the hollow section is bracketed with verses dealing with the fair treatment of women.

The theme of guidance is emphasized by the message to Christians that they are misguided in attributing otherness

to God and by the message to the Jews that they are misguided in believing that they could usurp the will of God
by killing one of His prophets. The theme of guidance is
reinforced by the mention of the path (God's way) in verses
137 and 175 which bracket this section.

Finally, the theme of monotheism, while being succinctly stated in the phrase "God is only one God" (4:171), is
laid out in greater detail at the outset of this section in the
following verse:

> You who believe, believe in God and His Messenger, as
> well as what He sent down before. Anyone who does not
> believe in God, His angels, His scriptures, His messen-
> gers, and the Last Day has gone far, far astray. (4:136)

Bibliography

EQ = *Encyclopedia of the Qur'an* (McAuliffe 2001-2006)

Abbott, H. Porter. 2008. *The Cambridge Introduction to Narrative*, 2nd edition. Cambridge, U.K.: Cambridge University Press.

Abdel Haleem, Muhammad A. S. 1999. *Understanding the Qur'an*. New York, NY: I. B. Tauris.

———. 2005. *The Qur'an: A New Translation*. Oxford, U.K.: Oxford University Press.

———. 2008. How to Read the Qur'an: *Surat al-Hadid* (*Q.* 57). *Journal of Qur'anic Studies* 10(2): 124-30.

Abdul-Raof, Hussein. 2003. Conceptual and Textual Chaining in Qur'anic Discourse. *Journal of Qur'anic Studies* 5(2): 72-94.

Abou El Fadl, Khaled. 2001. *Speaking in God's Name: Islamic Law, Authority and Women*. Oxford, U.K.: Oneworld.

Abu-Zahra, Nadia. 2001. Adultery and Fornication. *EQ* 1: 28-30.

Achrati, Ahmad. 2006. Deconstruction, Ethics and Islam. *Arabica* 53(4): 472-510.

———. 2008. Arabic, Qur'anic Speech and Postmodern Language: What the Qur'an Simply Says. *Arabica* 55: 161-203.

Adang, Camilla. 2001. Belief and Unbelief. *EQ* 1: 218-26.

———. 2002. Hypocrites and Hypocrisy. *EQ* 2: 468-72.

Afsaruddin, Asma. 2008. *The First Muslims: History and Memory*. Oxford, U.K.: Oneworld.

Ahmad, Kassim. 1997. *Hadith: A Re-evaluation*. Freemont, CA: Universal Unity.

Ahmed, Leila. 1992. *Women and Gender in Islam: Historical Roots of a Modern Debate*. New Haven, CT: Yale University Press.

Ahmed, Nafeez M. 2009. Our Terrorists. *New Internationalist* 426: 17-20.

Ahmed, Shahab. 2004. Satanic Verses. *EQ* 4: 531-35.

Alexander, Scott C. 2002. Fear. *EQ* 2: 194-98.

Ali, Ameer. 2007. The Closing of the Muslim Mind. *Journal of Muslim Minority Affairs* 27(3): 443-53.

Ali, Farhana and Jerrold Post. 2008. The History and Evolution of Martyrdom in the Service of Defensive Jihad: An Analysis of Suicide Bombers in Current Conflicts. *Social Research* 75(2): 615-54.

Ali, Kecia. 2006. "The Best of You Will Not Strike": Al-Shafi'i on Qur'an, Sunnah, and Wife-beating. *Comparative Islamic Studies* 2(2): 143-55.

Ali, Tariq. 2002. *The Clash of Fundamentalisms: Crusades, Jihads and Modernity*. London, U.K.: Verso.

Ali-Karamali, Sumbul. 2008. *The Muslim Next Door: The Qur'an, the Media, and that Veil Thing*. Ashland, OR: White Cloud Press.

Anees, Munawar A. 2006. Salvation and Suicide: What Does Islamic Theology Say? *Dialog: A Journal of Theology* 45(3): 275-79.

Arberry, Arthur. J. 1996. *The Koran Interpreted: A Translation*. New York, NY: Touchstone.

Arkoun, Mohammed. 2001. Contemporary Critical Practices and the Qur'an. *EQ* 1: 412-31.

Armstrong, Karen. 1991. *Muhammad*. London, U.K.: Orion House.

Aslan, Reza. 2005. *No God but God: The Origins, Evolution, and Future of Islam*. New York, NY: Random House.

Ataman, Kemal. 2007. Religion, Culture and the Shaping of Religious Attitudes: The Case of Islam. *Islam and Christian-Muslim Relations* 18(4): 495-508.

Bar-Asher, Meir M. 2004. Shi'ism and the Qur'an. *EQ* 4: 593-603.

Barazangi, Nimat H. 2004. *Woman's Identity and the Qur'an: A New Reading*. Gainesville, FL: University Press of Florida.

———. 2009. The Absence of Muslim Women in Shaping and Developing Islamic Thought. *Theological Review* 30: 155-82.

Barks, Coleman. 2004. *The Essential Rumi*, expanded edition. New York, NY: Harper Collins.

Barlas, Asma. 2002. *Believing Women in Islam: Unreading Patriarchal Readings of the Qur'an*. Austin, TX: University of Texas Press.

Basu, Kunal. 2003. *The Miniaturist*. London, U.K.: Weidenfeld & Nicolson.

Bauer, Karen. 2006. "Traditional" Exegeses of Q 4:34. *Comparative Islamic Studies* 2(2): 129-42.

Beekman, John, John Callow and Michael Kopesec. 1981. *The Semantic Structure of Written Communication*, 5th edition. Dallas, TX: Summer Institute of Linguistics.

Bell, Richard. 1926. *The Origin of Islam in its Christian Environment*. London, U.K.: Macmillan.

———. 1953. *Introduction to the Qur'an*. Edinburgh, U.K.: Edinburgh University Press.

Bellamy, James A. 2006. Textual Criticism of the Qur'an. *EQ* 5: 237-52.

Berg, Herbert. 2004. Polysemy in the Qur'an. *EQ* 4: 155-58.

Blair, Sheila S. 2008. *Islamic Calligraphy*. Edinburgh, U.K.: Edinburgh University Press.

Boullata, Issa J. 2003. Literary Structures of the Qur'an. *EQ* 3: 192-205.

Bowen, John R. 2008. *Why the French Don't Like Headscarves: Islam, the State, and Public Space*. Princeton, NJ: Princeton University Press.

Böwering, Gerhard. 2004. Prayer. *EQ* 4: 215-31.

Brockopp, Jonathan E. 2001. Concubines. *EQ* 1: 396-97.

Brown, Daniel W. 1996. *Rethinking Tradition in Modern Islamic Thought*. Cambridge, U.K.: Cambridge University Press.

Brown, Jonathan A. C. 2009. *Hadith: An Introduction*. Oxford, U.K.: Oneworld.

Bucaille, Maurice. 2003. *The Bible, the Qur'an and Science*. Elmhurst, NY: Tahrike Tarsile.

Burke, Jason. 2004. *Al-Qaeda: The True Story of Radical Islam*. New York, NY: I. B. Tauris.

Burton, John. 2001. Abrogation. *EQ* 1: 11-19.

Cabezon, Jose Ignacio. 2004. Identity and the Work of the Scholar of Religion. In *Identity and the Politics of Scholarship in the Study of Religion*, edited by Jose Ignacio Cabezon and Sheila Greeve Davaney, 43-60. New York, NY: Routledge.

Calvert, John. 2008. *Islamism: A Documentary and Reference Guide*. Westport, CT: Greenwood.

Campbell, Robert A. 2009. *Reading the Qur'an in English: An Introductory Guide*. Sydney, NS: Cape Breton University Press.

Chaudhry, Ayesha S. 2006. The Problem of Conscience and Hermeneutics: A Few Contemporary Approaches. *Comparative Islamic Studies* 2(2): 157-70.

Cleary, Thomas. 2004. *The Qur'an: A New Translation*. Burr Ridge, IL: Starlatch.

Cook, Michael. 2000. *The Koran: A Very Short Introduction*. Oxford, U.K.: Oxford University Press.

Crimp, Susan and Joel Richardson. 2008. *Why We Left Islam: Former Muslims Speak Out*. Los Angeles, CA: WND Books.

Crone, Patricia. 2006. War. *EQ* 5: 455-59.

Cumper, Peter and Tom Lewis. 2009. Taking Religion Seriously? Human Rights and Hijab in Europe—Some Problems of Adjudication. *Journal of Law & Religion* 24(2): 599-627.

Darrow, William R. 2003. Magians. *EQ* 3: 244-45.

De Blois, Francois. 2004. Sabians. *EQ* 4: 511-13.

Elias, Jamal J. 2003. Light. *EQ* 3: 186-87.

Elmarsafy, Ziad. 2009a. Manifesto for a New Translation of the Qur'an: The Politics of "Respect" and the End(s) of Orientalism. Paper delivered at "Britain and the Muslim World: Historical Perspectives," University of Exeter, 17-19 April.

———. 2009b. *The Enlightenment Qur'an: The Politics of Translation and the Construction of Islam*. Oxford, U.K.: Oneworld.

Ernst, Carl W. 2003. *Following Muhammad: Rethinking Islam in the Contemporary World*. Chapel Hill, NC: University of North Carolina Press.

Fadel, Mohammad. 2003. Murder. *EQ* 3: 458-60.

Fadiman, James, and Robert Freger, 1997. *Essential Sufism*. New York, NY: Harper Collins.

Faizer, Rizwi. 2002. Expeditions and Battles. *EQ* 2: 143-52.

Farrin, Raymond K. 2010. Surat al-Baqarah: A Structural Analysis. *The Muslim World* 100: 17-32.

Firestone, Reuven. 1996. Conceptions of Holy War in Biblical and Qur'anic Tradition. *Journal of Religious Ethics* 24(1): 99-123.

———. 2001. Abraham. *EQ* 1: 5-10.

Frolov, Dmitry V. 2004. Path or Way. *EQ* 4: 28-31.

———. 2006. Stoning. *EQ* 5: 129-30.

Fukuyama, Francis. 1992. *The End of History and the Last Man*. New York, NY: Free Press.

Gabriel, Mark A. 2002. *Islam and Terrorism*. Lake Mary, FL: Charisma House.

Gätje, Helmut. 1996. *The Qur'an and its Exegesis: Selected Texts with Classical and Modern Muslim Interpretations*. Oxford, U.K.: Oneworld.

Ghattas, Raouf and Carol B. Ghattas. 2009. *A Christian Guide to the Qur'an: Building Bridges in Muslim Evangelism*. Grand Rapids, MI: Kregel.

Gilliot, Claude. 2002. Exegesis of the Qur'an: Classical and Medieval. *EQ* 2: 99-124.

Goldziher, Ignaz. 1981. *Introduction to Islamic Theology and Law*. Trans. by Andras and Ruth Hamori. Princeton, NJ: Princeton University Press.

Gorman, Michael. 2001. *Elements of Biblical Exegesis: A Basic Guide for Students and Ministers*. Peabody, MA: Hendrickson.

Gracia, Jorge J. E. 1995. *A Theory of Textuality: The Logic and Epistemology*. Albany, NY: SUNY Press.

———. 1996. *Texts: Ontological Status, Identity, Author, Audience*. Albany, NY: SUNY Press.

———. 2000. Relativism and the Interpretation of Texts. *Metaphilosophy* 31(1/2): 43-62.

Gregorson, Niels Henrik. 2009. Taboos: The Danish Cartoon Crisis 2005-2008. *Dialog* 48(1): 79-96.

Griffith, Sidney H. 2001. Christians and Christianity. *EQ* 1: 307-16.

Günther, Sebastian. 2001. Bloodshed. *EQ* 1: 240-41.

Gwynne, Rosalind. 2006. Usama bin Ladin, the Qur'an and Jihad. *Religion* 36: 61-90.

Hallaq, Wael B. 1997. *A History of Islamic Legal Theories: An Introduction to Sunni usul al-fiqh*. Cambridge, U.K.: Cambridge University Press.

———. 2001. Apostasy. *EQ* 1: 119-22.

———. 2003. Law and the Qur'an. *EQ* 3: 149-72.

Hammer, Juliane. 2008. Identity, Authority, and Activism: American Muslim Women Approach the Qur'an. *The Muslim World* 98: 443-64.

Harmon, Stephen A. 2008. Joseph and Pharaoh: Religious Fundamentalist and Secular Modernists in Contemporary Islam and Their Hostility towards Western Liberalism. *Midwest Quarterly* 49(2): 179-99.

Hawting, Gerald R. 2002a. Idolatry and Idolaters. *EQ* 2: 475-80.

———. 2002b. Idols and Images. *EQ* 2: 481-84.

———. 2003. Ka'ba. *EQ* 3: 75-79.

———. 2004. Pilgrimage. *EQ* 4: 91-100.

Heath, Jennifer, ed. 2008. *The Veil: Women Writers on Its History, Lore, and Politics*. Berkeley, CA: University of California Press.

Heath, Peter. 2003. Metaphor. *EQ* 3: 384-88.

Hilali, Muhammad and Muhammad Khan. 1997. *Translation of the Meanings of the Noble Quran in the English Language*. Madina, Saudi Arabia: King Fahd Complex.

Hoffman, Bruce. 2006. *Inside Terrorism*, rev. and exp. ed. New York, NY: Columbia University Press.

Huntington, Samuel P. 1998. *The Clash of Civilizations and the Remaking of World Order*. New York, NY: Simon & Schuster.

Ibn Hisham, Abd al-Malik. 1955. *The Life of Muhammad: A Translation of Ishaq's Sirat Rasul Allah*. Trans. by Alfred Guillaume. Oxford, U.K.: Oxford University Press.

Ibn Warraq. 1995. *Why I Am Not a Muslim*. Amherst, NY: Prometheus Books.

Jansen, Johannes J. G. 1986. *The Neglected Duty: The Creed of Sadat's Assassins and Islamic Resurgence in the Middle East*. New York, NY: MacMillan.

Jarrar, Maher. 2002. Houris. *EQ* 2: 456-57.

Jenssen, Herbjorn. 2001. Arabic Language. *EQ* 1: 127-35.

Jones, Alan. 2007. *The Qur'an*. Exeter, U.K.: Gibb Memorial Trust.

Jones, Sherry. 2008. *The Jewel of Medina*. New York, NY: Beaufort.

Juergensmeyer, Mark. 2003. *Terror in the Mind of God: The Global Rise of Religious Violence*, 3rd edition. Berkeley, CA: University of California Press.

Juschka, Darlene, ed. 2001. *Feminism in the Study of Religion: A Reader*. New York, NY: Continuum.

Juynboll, Gautier H. A. 2002. Hadith and the Qur'an. *EQ* 2: 376-97.

Kadi, Wadad, and Mustansir Mir. 2003. Literature and the Qur'an. *EQ* 3: 205-27.

Kamali, Mohammad H. 2003. *Principles of Islamic Jurisprudence*, 3rd edition. Cambridge, U.K.: Islamic Text Society.

———. 2008. *Shari'ah: An Introduction*. Oxford, U.K.: Oneworld.

Kassis, Hanna E. 1983. *A Concordance of the Qur'an*. Berkeley, CA: University of California Press.

Kepel, Gilles. 2002. *Jihad: The Trail of Political Islam*. Cambridge, MA: Harvard University Press.

Kinberg, Leah. 2001. Ambiguous. *EQ* 1: 70-76.

Küng, Hans. 2007. *Islam: Past, Present and Future*. Oxford, U.K.: Oneworld.

Landau-Tasseron, Ella. 2003. Jihad. *EQ* 3: 35-42.

Lawrence, Bruce. 2006. *The Qur'an: A Biography*. London, U.K.: Atlantic Books.

Lawson, Todd. 2009. *The Crucifixion and the Qur'an: A Study in the History of Muslim Thought*. Oxford, U.K.: Oneworld.

Leaman, Oliver. 2004. *Islamic Aesthetics: An Introduction*. Notre Dame, IL: University of Notre Dame Press.

Leehmuis, Frederick. 2001. Codices of the Qur'an. *EQ* 1: 347-51.

Lings, Martin. 1983. *Muhammad*. Richmond, VT: Inner Traditions International.

Lowry, Joseph. 2004. The Reception of al-Shafi'i's Concept of *Amr* and *Nahy* in the Thought of His Student al-Muzani. In *Law and Education in Medieval Islam: Studies in Memory of Professor George Makdisi*, edited by Joseph Lowry, Devin J. Stewart and Shawkat M. Toorawa, 128-49. Exeter, U.K.: Gibb Memorial Trust.

Madigan, Daniel A. 2001. Book. *EQ* 1: 242-51.

———. 2004. Revelation and Inspiration. *EQ* 4: 437-47.

Mahmoud, Mohamed. 2006. To Beat or Not To Beat: On the Exegetical Dilemmas over Qur'an, 4:34. *Journal of the American Oriental Society* 126(4): 537-50.

Mandaville, Peter. 2007. Globalization and the Politics of Religious Knowledge: Pluralizing Authority in the Muslim World. *Theory, Culture & Society* 24(2): 101-15.

Martin, Richard C. 2002. Inimitability. *EQ* 2: 526-35.

Mattson, Ingrid. 2008. *The Story of the Qur'an: Its History and Place in Muslim Life*. Oxford, U.K.: Blackwell.

McAuliffe, Jane Dammen, ed. 2001-2006. *Encyclopedia of the Qur'an*, 5 volumes. Leiden, Netherlands: Brill.

Menocal, Maria R. 2003. *The Ornament of the World: How Muslims, Jews, and Christians Created a Culture of Tolerance in Medieval Spain*. Boston, MA: Back Bay Books.

Mernissi, Fatima. 1995. *Women and Islam: An Historical and Theological Enquiry*, trans. by Mary Jo Lakeland. Oxford, U.K.: Blackwell.

Michalak, Laurence and Karen Trocki. 2006. Alcohol and Islam: An Overview. *Contemporary Drug Problems* 33: 523-62.

Mir, Mustansir. 1986. *Coherence in the Qur'an: A Study of Islahi's Concept of Nazm in Taddabur-i Qur'an*. Indianapolis, IN: American Trust Publications.

———. 1988. The Qur'an as Literature. *Religion & Literature* 20(1): 49-64.

———. 2008. *Understanding the Islamic Scripture: A Study of Selected Passages from the Qur'an*. New York, NY: Pearson.

Momen, Moojan. 1985. *An Introduction to Shi'i Islam: The History and Doctrines of Twelver Shi'ism*. New Haven, CT: Yale University Press.

Morgan, Elizabeth. 2005. Mary and Modesty. *Christianity and Literature* 54(2): 209-33.

Morgan, Michael H. 2007. *Lost History: The Enduring Legacy of Muslim Scientists, Thinkers, and Artisans*. Washington, DC: National Geographic.

Motzki, Harald. 2003. Marriage and Divorce. *EQ* 3: 276-81

Mozaffari, Mehdi. 2007. What is Islamism? History and Definition of a Concept. *Totalitarian Movements and Political Religions* 8(1): 17-33.

Mubarak, Hadia. 2004. Breaking the Interpretive Monopoly: A Re-examination of Verse 4:34. *Hawwa* 2(3): 261-89.

Murata, Sachiko and William C. Chittick. 1994. *The Vision of Islam*. St. Paul, MN: Paragon House.

Nanji, Azim. 2001. Almsgiving. *EQ* 1: 64-70.

Nelson, Kristina. 2001. *The Art of Reciting the Qur'an*. Cairo, Egypt: American University in Cairo Press.

Neuwirth, Angelika. 1981. *Studien Zur Komposition Der Mekkanischen Suren*. Berlin, Germany: De Gruyter.

———. 2002. Form and Structure of the Qur'an. *EQ* 2: 245-66.

———. 2004a. Ramadan. *EQ* 4: 338-48.

———. 2004b. Rhetoric and the Qur'an. *EQ* 4: 461-76.

Omar, Abdul M. 2003. *Dictionary of the Holy Qur'an*. Rhein-
felden, Germany: Noor Foundation.

Palmer, Richard E. 1969. *Hermeneutics: Interpretation Theory in
Schleiermacher, Dilthey, Heidegger and Gadamer*. Evanston,
IL: Northwestern University Press.

Pamuk, Orhan. 2001. *My Name is Red*. New York, NY: Vintage Books.

Powers, David S. 2002. Inheritance. *EQ* 2: 518-26.

Qutb, Sayyid. 1967. *This Religion of Islam*. Palo Alto, CA: Al-
Manar Press.

Rahman, Fazlur. 1982. *Islam and Modernity: Transformation of an Intellectual Tradition*. Chicago, IL: University of Chicago Press.

———. 1994. *Major Themes in the Qur'an*. Minneapolis, MN:
Bibliotheca Islamica.

Ramadan, Tariq. 2007. *In the Footsteps of the Prophet: Lessons from the
Life of Muhammad*. Oxford, U.K.: Oxford University Press.

Raven, Wim. 2003. Martyrs. *EQ* 3: 281-87.

———. 2006. Sira and the Qur'an. *EQ* 5: 29-51.

Reda, Nevin. 2010. Holistic Approaches to the Qur'an: A Historical Background. *Religion Compass* 5(8): 495-506.

Rippin, Andrew. 2002. Foreign Vocabulary. *EQ* 2: 226-37.

———. 2003. Occasions of Revelation. *EQ* 3: 569-72.

———. 2006. Witness to Faith. *EQ* 5: 488-91.

Robinson, Neal. 2001. Crucifixion. *EQ* 1: 487-89.

———. 2003a. *Discovering the Qur'an*, 2nd edition. Washington,
DC: Georgetown University Press.

———. 2003b. Jesus. *EQ* 3: 7-20.

Roded, Ruth. 2006. Women and the Qur'an. *EQ* 5: 523-41.

Rodinson, Maxime. 1980. *Muhammad*. New York, NY: Free Press.

Rowson, Everett K. 2002. Homosexuality. *EQ* 2: 444-45.

Rubin, Uri. 2001. Children of Israel. *EQ* 1: 303-07.

———. 2002. Hafsa. *EQ* 2: 397-98.

———. 2003. Jews and Judaism. *EQ* 3: 21-34.

Rushdie, Salman. 1988. *The Satanic Verses*. London, U.K.: Viking
Press.

Rustomji, Nerina. 2007. American Visions of the *Houri*. *The MuslimWorld* 97: 79-92.

Sachedina, Abdulaziz. 2001. *The Islamic Roots of Democratic Pluralism*. New York, NY: Oxford University Press.

Saeed, Abdullah. 2006. *Interpreting the Qur'an: Towards a Contemporary Approach*. London, U.K.: Routledge.

———. 2008a. *Introduction to the Qur'an: History, Interpretation, and Approaches*. London, U.K.: Routledge.

———. 2008b. Some Reflections on the Contextualist Approach to Ethico-legal Studies of the Qur'an. *Bulletin of the School of Oriental and African Studies* 71(2): 221-37.

Sale, George. 1921. *The Koran*. London, U.K.: Frederick Warne.

Sardar, Ziauddin, Sohail Inayatullah and Gail Boxwell. 2003. *Islam, Postmodernism, and Other Futures: A Ziauddin Sardar Reader*. London, U.K.: Pluto Press.

Schacht, Joseph. 1964. *An Introduction to Islamic Law*. Oxford, U.K.: Clarendon Press.

Schmidtke, Sabine. 2001. Creeds. *EQ* 1: 480-85.

Scott, Rachel M. 2009. A Contextual Approach to Women's Rights in the Qur'an: Readings of 4:34. *The MuslimWorld* 99: 60-85.

Sells, Michael. 1999. *Approaching the Qur'an: The Early Revelations*. Ashland, OR: White Cloud Press.

Shapiro, James S. 2000. *Oberammergau: The Troubling Story of the World's Most Famous Passion Play*. New York, NY: Pantheon.

Sharon, Moshe. 2004. People of the Book. *EQ* 4: 36-43.

Shirazi, Faegheh. 2001. *The Veil Unveiled: The Hijab in Modern Culture*. Gainesville, FL: University Press of Florida.

Silvers, Laury. 2006. "In the Book We Have Left Out Nothing": The Ethical Problem of the Existence of Verse 4:34 in the Qur'an. *Comparative Islamic Studies* 2(2): 171-80.

Spellberg, Denise A. 2001. Aisha bint Abi Bakr. *EQ* 1: 55-60.

Spencer, Robert. 2005. *The Politically Incorrect Guide to Islam and the Crusades*. Washington, DC: Regnery Publishing.

Stewart, Devin J. 2001. Blasphemy. *EQ* 1: 235-36.

———. 2004. Sex and Sexuality. *EQ* 4: 580-85.

Stowasser, Barbara F. 1997. The Hijab: How a Curtain Became an Institution and a Cultural Symbol. In *Humanism, Culture & Language in the Near East: Studies in Honor of Georg Krotkoff*, edited by Asma Afsaruddin and A. H. Mathias Zahniser, 87-104. Winona Lake, IN: Eisenbrauns.

———. 2006. Wives of the Prophet. *EQ* 5: 506-21.

Thomas, David. 2006. Trinity. *EQ* 5: 368-72.

Torrey, Charles C. 1933. *The Jewish Foundation of Islam*. New York, NY: Jewish Institute of Religion Press.

Toynbee, Arnold J. 1948. *Civilization on Trial*. Oxford, U.K.: Oxford University Press.

Trask, Robert L. 2000. *The Penguin Dictionary of English Grammar*. New York, NY: Penguin.

Vasalou, Sophia. 2002. The Miraculous Eloquence of the Qur'an: General Trajectories and Individual Approaches. *Journal of Qur'anic Studies* 4(2): 23-53.

Waardenburg, Jacques. 2001. Death and the Dead. *EQ* 1: 505-11.

Wadud, Amina. 2006. *Inside the Gender Jihad: Women's Reform in Islam*. Oxford, U.K.: Oneworld.

Wagemakers, Joas. 2008. Defining the Enemy: Abu Muhammad al-Maqdisi's Radical Reading of *Surat al-Mumtahana*. *Die Welt des Islams* 48: 348-71.

Wagner, Walter H. 2008. *Opening the Qur'an: Introducing Islam's Holy Book*. Notre Dame, IN: University of Notre Dame Press.

Wagtendonk, Kees. 2002. Fasting. *EQ* 2: 180-84.

Wallace-Murphy, Tim. 2006. *What Islam Did For Us: Understanding Islam's Contribution to Western Civilization*. London, U.K.: Watkins.

Walton, Douglas. 1999. The Fallacy of Many Questions: On the Notions of Complexity, Loadedness and Unfair Entrapment in Interrogative Theory. *Argumentation* 13(4): 379-83.

Webb, Gisela, ed. 2000. *Windows of Faith: Muslim Women Scholar-Activists in North America*. Syracuse, NY: Syracuse University Press.

Wielandt, Rotraud. 2002. Exegesis of the Qur'an: Early Modern and Contemporary. *EQ* 2: 124-42.

Wilde, Clare and Jane Dammen McAuliffe. 2004. Religious Pluralism in the Qur'an. *EQ* 4: 398-419.

Williams, Juliet A. 2009. Unholy Matrimony? Feminism, Orientalism, and the Possibility of Double Critique. *Signs* 34(3): 611-32.

Yuksel, Edip, Layth S. Al-Shaiban and Martha Schulte-Nafeh. 2007. *Quran: A Reformist Translation*. Tucson, AZ: Brainbow Press.

Yusuf Ali, Abdullah. 2004. *The Meaning of the Holy Qur'an*, 11th edition. Beltsville, MD: Amana Publications.

Zahniser, A. H. Mathias. 1997. Sura as Guidance and Exhortation: The Composition of *Surat al-Nisa*. In *Humanism, Culture & Language in the Near East: Studies in Honor of Georg Krotkoff*, edited by Asma Afsaruddin and A. H. Mathias Zahniser, 71-85. Winona Lake, IN: Eisenbrauns.

Zebiri, Kate. 2003. Towards a Rhetorical Criticism of the Qur'an. *Journal of Qur'anic Studies* 5(2): 95-120.

Index of Subjects

Abraham, 3, 159, 179, 180, 188, 192, 195

abrogation, 8, 53-56, 116, 173, 186

Abu Bakr, 56, 82, 83

adultery, 7, 49, 82, 83, 90-94, 107

afterlife, 5, 71, 138, 174, 184,189

Aisha, 27, 81-85

Ali ibn Abi Talib, 83,182

al-Arabi, 25, 111, 114

al-Shafiʻi, 50, 112, 113

al-Suyuti, 25, 55

al-Tabari, 24, 109

ambiguity, 36, 91, 136, 141

analogy, 50-52, 112

apostasy, 160, 172

articulation, 7, 17, 19, 20, 182

atomistic, 36, 57

authenticity, 13, 38, 39, 42, 108, 111

authority, 1, 13, 22, 24, 25, 32, 37, 39, 41, 42, 44, 45, 50, 52,
    58, 86, 89, 109, 112, 140, 150, 167, 172, 198

ayahs, 11, 15

basmalah, 25, 62, 69, 156

battle, 7, 60, 66, 72, 83, 84,86, 130-133, 136, 139, 141-156,
    167, 172, 174

Battle Gains, 156

bearing witness, 182

believers, 8, 41, 71, 79, 84, 86, 87, 123, 126, 127, 131, 146,
    147, 149, 151, 171, 174-189, 192, 196

blasphemy, 172

caliph, 13, 83, 85, 88, 92

canonization, 13, 108

chiasm, 33, 64-66
Christians, 3, 8, 16, 18, 24, 143, 155, 167, 173, 189-193,
    195, 199
codification, 13
coherence, 15, 59, 159
commentary, 8, 36, 192
commentaries, 1, 8, 19, 22-26, 36, 163, 192, 203
community, 7, 16, 17, 20, 24, 37, 47, 48, 50, 52, 54, 58, 59,
    74, 82, 85, 98, 103, 116, 131, 132, 136, 139, 142,
    146, 151, 171, 172, 175, 183-185, 193
companions, 24, 28, 37, 52, 56, 71
concatenation, 33, 63, 174
context, 1-4, 6, 8, 10, 12, 14, 16, 18-20, 22, 24, 26-28, 30,
    32-34, 36, 38-40, 42, 44-46, 48, 50, 52-54, 56, 58,
    60, 62, 64, 66, 73, 78, 83, 95, 97, 117, 118, 120, 122,
    131, 132, 136-138, 147, 159, 165, 166, 197
contextualist, 29, 30, 33, 37, 39, 41, 116, 117
co-text, 33, 34, 37, 78, 117, 138, 152
crucifixion, 8, 173, 206-209
dancing, 8, 173, 204
David, 72, 142, 189
disbelievers, 65, 66, 74, 157, 162
divorce, 7, 72, 74-76, 81, 85, 86, 104
Egypt, 14, 24, 26, 29, 41, 57, 69, 86, 141, 160, 193
exegesis, 12, 18-24, 26, 54, 118
explanation, 17-19, 22, 29, 51, 134, 156, 162
fard, 47, 48
fasting, 48, 71, 75, 86, 182, 185, 186
fighting, 83, 133, 139, 141, 143, 144, 146, 147, 149-153,
    158, 162, 167
fundamentalism, 114, 135

Gospel, 3, 189

grammar, 17, 24, 33

guidance, 5, 6, 47, 49, 51, 53, 56, 112, 133, 181, 204, 208, 209

hadith, 11, 24, 28, 37-39, 49-51, 88, 92, 108, 110, 111, 113, 156, 158-160, 165, 166, 177, 178, 183, 190, 198, 203

hajj, 38, 150, 151, 182, 187

halal, 49

Hanafi, 29, 46, 48

hanif, 179

haram, 47

harb, 132, 133

Hell, 32, 65, 66, 140, 165, 166, 174

hermeneutics, 12, 17, 20-22

hijab, 7, 11, 68, 87, 116, 125-129, 175

hijra, 11, 14

houris, 167-170

hypocrites, 6, 8, 50, 62, 65, 66, 139, 140, 147, 158, 171-209

Ibn Kathir, 25, 109

Ibn Taymiyya, 25, 36, 163, 165

idolatry, 4, 8, 145, 148, 149, 173, 195-197, 199, 208, 209

ijma, 50, 52

ijtihad, 53, 54

iltifat, 34

inheritance, 68, 72, 73, 78, 89, 97, 122

inimitability, 18, 33, 35, 51, 53

India, 26, 46

inductive, 59, 64

intermediary, 21, 24, 60, 63, 195, 196

interpretation, 3, 5, 8, 10-12, 15-22, 24-26, 28, 29, 34, 36-
    39, 41, 44, 47, 50, 52-54, 56, 57, 61, 62, 67, 71, 83,
    88, 94-96, 99, 102, 104, 106-114, 117, 119, 121,
    123, 124, 135, 139, 143, 148, 149, 155, 156, 165,
    168, 188, 197
intertextuality, 37
intoxication, 8, 52, 173, 199-206
Iron, 165
Isaac, 169, 179
Ishmael, 179, 188
isnad, 38
Jesus, 3, 8, 68, 83, 126, 155, 173, 189, 193-195, 206-208
Jews, 3, 8, 16, 18, 24, 145, 155, 172, 173, 183, 186, 189-
    193, 199, 206-208
jihad, 7, 11, 40, 53, 132-134, 137, 144, 150, 157-160, 163,
    165, 166
Joseph, 39, 69, 112
judgment, 5, 6, 16, 33, 46, 48, 69, 134, 178, 191, 196, 208,
    209
juz, 12, 13
Khadija, 81, 82, 84
Kharijis, 25
killing, 7, 58, 132, 136-141, 145, 151, 155, 161
kitab, 112, 113, 190
language, 2, 10, 17-21, 30-33, 35, 37, 43, 61, 98, 107, 133,
    169, 170
laylat al-qadr, 186
law, 32, 45, 46, 51, 54, 89, 111, 112, 125, 156, 159, 189
legal, 23-25, 39, 45-49, 51, 72, 89, 109, 111, 113, 117, 120,
    129, 137, 160, 199
lewdness, 7, 68, 90-93

linguistics, 10, 24, 33
literal, 2, 19, 23, 63, 95, 113, 126, 171, 180
literary, 12, 19, 27, 33, 34, 42, 59, 63, 94, 170, 199
Lot, 84, 93, 94, 125, 127, 192
Luqman, 16, 196
Madina, 14, 57, 58, 82, 86, 87, 135, 136, 139, 144, 146, 147,
        150, 159, 171, 183, 186, 192, 206
Makkah, 4, 14, 82, 135, 136, 143, 144, 146, 148, 151, 152,
        159, 182, 183, 185, 187, 196-198
makruh, 47
mandub, 47
marriage, 7, 24, 68, 72, 74-89, 91, 104, 105, 110, 113, 121,
        122
martyr, 161, 167, 168, 205
Mary, 68, 83, 84, 126, 195, 207, 208
matn, 38
metaphor, 18, 37, 63, 180
migration, 14, 135, 146
monotheism, 5, 6, 8, 146, 179, 180, 208, 209
Moses, 3, 179, 186, 189, 192, 195
mubah, 47
mufti, 111, 112
Muhammad, 1, 3, 9, 13-15, 20, 23, 26, 27, 37, 38, 41, 56,
        81-87, 108, 112, 115, 116, 142, 143, 147, 148, 150,
        154, 160, 161, 164-166, 169, 172, 175, 177-179,
        182, 186, 190, 195, 19, 198
murder, 7, 112, 132, 136, 138, 167
music, 8, 173
Mutazilis, 36
narrative, 23, 27, 31, 57, 61-63, 69
naskh, see abrogation

orphans, 58, 68, 71, 78, 92

Osama bin Laden, 163, 164

orthodox, 24, 36, 41, 173, 177, 194

orthopraxy, 177

Paradise, 71, 94, 160, 167, 168, 170

parallelism, 33, 65, 90, 121-123

paraphrastic, 23

philosophical, 12, 21, 25, 46, 181

photography, 92, 199

pilgrimage, 75, 87, 151, 152, 182, 186-188

prayer, 2, 10, 18, 43, 48, 49, 92, 152, 182-184

prophets, 8, 182, 195, 198

Psalms, 3, 92, 189

punishment, 7, 48, 49, 55, 70, 83, 90, 92-94, 99, 100, 103, 104, 106, 120, 123, 124, 137, 138, 140, 142, 178

qiyas, 50, 51

qital, 132, 150, 157

Qutb, Sayyid, 28, 136, 160

recitation, 1, 12, 13, 17, 18, 32, 39, 61, 65, 183, 198, 199, 205

Repentance, 155

reward, 1, 36, 48, 49, 53, 71, 147, 151, 160, 161, 167, 168, 170, 178, 184

rhetorical, 17, 34, 36, 42, 77, 95, 117, 121, 134, 175

Risalah, 50, 112, 113.

Rumi, 204

sacred, 1, 2, 3, 10, 32, 143, 145, 151, 152, 155, 183, 187

salat, see prayer

Satan, 50, 68, 161, 197, 198

sawm, see fasting

science, 4, 12, 22, 25-27, 107, 125, 129

scripture, 3, 9, 14, 16, 18, 35, 50, 54, 68, 93, 136, 145, 158, 190, 192

sectarian, 25, 83

secular, 89, 161

shahadah, 50, 182

shahid, see martyr

shariah, 6, 11, 45-47, 49-56

Shia, 25, 38, 46, 83, 88, 166, 167, 182, 183, 205

shirk, 50, 195

sira, 37, 50, 67, 124, 127, 181

sirat, 181

structure, 6, 7, 9, 14, 31, 33, 50, 57-60, 64, 65, 77, 80, 91, 98, 188

successors, 24, 37, 50, 52, 172

symmetry, 60, 169

Sufi, 8, 25, 173, 181, 204

sunnah, 11, 37, 50, 51, 53, 54, 112, 159

Sunni, 24, 25, 36, 38, 48, 83, 88

tafsir, 19, 22, 23, 50

tajwid, see recitation

taqwa, 50, 161, 178

tawil, 22, 23, 50

temporary marriage, 50, 74, 87-89

terrorism, 7, 50, 71, 133, 137, 139, 159-163, 165-170

textualist, 29

The Cow, 12, 16, 57

The Family of Imran, 56

The Hypocrites, 174

The Opening, 12, 110, 150, 181, 183

thematic, 6, 7, 15, 16, 26, 28, 29, 31, 57-60, 62-66, 120-122, 159 theology, 1, 5, 25, 27, 32, 191

Torah, 3, 50, 65, 68, 141, 179, 189, 192

translation, 3, 9, 11, 17, 19, 20, 25, 31-33, 38, 40, 43, 57, 58, 77, 88, 91, 95, 101, 102, 104, 106, 107, 149, 150, 157, 169, 175, 193

travel, 104

Trinity, 104, 135, 194, 208, 209

Umar, 56, 81, 85, 88, 92

umra, see pilgrimage

unbelievers, 41, 126, 162, 167, 171, 188, 189, 192

Uthman, 13, 86

veiling, 125-127, 130

virgins, 104, 129, 167, 169, 170

wajib, 47, 48

war, 4, 6, 7, 10, 15, 28, 34-36, 40, 42, 48-50, 53, 63, 65, 66, 69-71, 74, 77-79, 82, 83, 85, 86, 88, 93, 95, 98, 99, 104, 131-173, 175, 177, 178, 180, 181, 184, 190-192, 196, 198

water, 45-47, 104, 184

wife beating, 7, 68, 94-126

wine, 52, 119, 200-205

witnesses, 72, 83, 90, 92, 112, 119, 122, 172, 174, 177, 182

wives of Muhammad, 79-87

women, 6, 7, 42-44, 56, 58, 60-62, 66-82, 84, 86-90, 92-94, 96-98, 100-102, 104-114, 116, 118-120, 122, 124-130, 165, 167, 168, 184, 199, 208, 209

Women Tested, 165

zakat, see almsgiving